Daddy's Long Goodbye

DADDY'S LONG GOODBYE

Darlene Machtan

Mach10 Publishing
Rhinelander, WI

DADDY'S LONG GOODBYE. Copyright © 2020 by Darlene Machtan. All rights reserved. No part of this publication may be reproduced, stored or transmitted in any form or by any means, electronic, mechanical, photocopying, recording, scanning, or otherwise without written permission from the publisher. It is illegal to copy this book, post it to a website, or distribute it by any other means without permission.

Published in the United States by Mach10 Publishing.

Photograph credits:

Pages 1, 7, 59, 73, 93, 121, 159, 221, 223 and Jacket © Darlene Machtan.

Page 213 Red-winged blackbird (Agelaius phoeniceus) in tidal marsh, Galveston, Texas, USA © Ivan Kuzmin/Shutterstock.com.

ISBN 978-1-7344758-1-4 (pbk)

ISBN 978-1-7344758-0-7 (ebook)

Printed in the United States of America

Book design by Nan Andrews

Publisher caricature by Jim Makris, page 5. Used with permission.

10 9 8 7 6 5 4 3 2 1

First edition: February 2020

Mach10 Publishing
Rhinelander, WI

Contents

Dedication
xiii

Prologue
Daddy's Girl
3

First Fall and Winter

The Decision
9

The Transition
16

The Drive
19

Going to the Dogs
23

Learning to Dance
27

No More Driving
30

Second Opinion
33

Asking for Help
35

The Schedule
37

Always on Sunday
40

White Trash TV
47
It's in the Cards
51
Dancing Again
53
On the Road
56

Spring
A Place in the Sun
61
Never Forgotten
63

Summer
Glad All Over
75
Flying High
79
On the Road Again
82
Accordions, All Girl Rock Band, and Daddy
86
The Summer of Love and Fitness
91

Fall, Winter, Spring, Summer, and Fall
The Honeymoon is Over
95
Taking a Break--Almost
100

Celebrating Ninety Years
106

Settling in to Change
109

Time for a Break
111

It All Depends
113

Point of No Return
117

Year Two

Finding Grace
123

Finding Words
127

Resolution
130

Preparations
135

Happy 91st Birthday
139

The First Weekend
142

The Adjustment
146

Cards
151

More Cards
153

A Period of Grace
155

Final Winter

Puerta Vallarta
161

The Real Deal
162

The Body Bag
164

The Beginning of the Decline
166

Hospice
171

Dwindling
175

Nancy
177

Glad All Over
180

Affirmation
182

More Company
184

Easter
187

Monday and Tuesday
188

Another Step, Another Breath
192

The W(h)iners' Farewell
198

Just Like That
201

The Devil Is in the Details
205

Moving Out
209

The Return of Spring
Letting Go
215

I'll Fly Away
217

(In)Visibility
220

About the Author
221

Acknowledgements
222

Dedication

For Daddy:

"I know it's not much,

but it's the best I can do.

My gift is my song,

and this one's for you."

from "Your Song"

by Elton John and Bernie Taupin

PROLOGUE

Daddy's Girl, Summer 2012

Daddy's Girl

"Daddy's Girl." Those words have followed me as long as I can remember. Even though I am now sixty-four, my brothers still occasionally launch them at me across the living room like hand grenades, and there is no way to dodge them and no place to hide. I suppose having carried this title since birth, it was inevitable that it would be I who would volunteer to care for my father when he could no longer live alone. Our bond began before I was even born.

Mom and Dad were busily raising three sons when I was conceived. Cliff was eight, Glenn was six, and Dale was four. When Daddy found out Mom was pregnant again, he said, "This one's a girl. I know it." He was so convinced that he had a daughter on the way that he bet his buddy at the local tavern a case of beer that I'd be a girl. Months later when I was born shortly after midnight, all girl despite my weighing in at a whopping ten pounds, thirteen ounces, Daddy was elated. He immediately headed to the tavern to claim his case of beer and bragging rights, only to discover to his great dismay that the bar had closed before he could get there. That didn't diminish his glee in handing out "It's a Girl" cigars at every subsequent opportunity.

It is hard to say why he was so delighted by a daughter.

He and Mom ran a dairy farm in Central Wisconsin together, and there was plenty of physical labor that sons were perhaps better equipped to do. Maybe I made up for the sister he never had—who knows? It didn't hurt that I liked to be outdoors with him while he did his chores. "Come keep me company, Sissy," he'd say, and off we'd go to fix fence or plant corn or get the cows. We never talked much, though. Daddy wasn't a talker. My presence seemed to be enough.

My brothers recognized that I was his favorite, and they were not amused. They resented my lofty status, and they taunted me regularly when Dad was out of earshot. I never got used to it, so somewhere along the line I think that I decided if they wanted me to be a boy so much, I'd act like one. By the time my brother Ken was born two years later, I was well on my way to tomboy status. That only seemed to further endear me to Daddy, which rankled my brothers even more. As the baby of the family, Ken was clearly Mom's favorite, but nobody except me appeared to notice that. For the most part he escaped the wrath of my siblings, and Ken and I were close, but from time to time he'd join the rest of my brothers in their annoying mocking singsong chant of "Daddy's Girl."

I honestly don't remember favoritism on my dad's part. I know that he liked to spend time with me, but I don't ever remember going anywhere special with him, receiving money or gifts, or even hearing much in the way of compliments. I don't think he talked to me more than anyone else, and he wasn't one to give advice. What was it that everyone else saw between us that I didn't? I'm still not sure. Maybe it was simply his great delight that I was born female.

Daddy didn't call or write or visit when I moved away for college. That wasn't his way. But he loved my weekends at home, and he waited until I returned each Christmas break to go shopping for Mom's Christmas present, just as we had always done. He continued to wait for me to join him in his Christmas shopping as long as Mom was alive. He was perfectly capable of doing this shopping by himself; he just liked the ritual of going together.

As I grew older and moved away to start a marriage and career of my own, Daddy and I grew apart a bit. I was busy with my own life and not returning home as regularly as I once had. We were still on good terms, but Mom's health was steadily failing, and my focus was on her. It wasn't until after Mom died, and Daddy was truly on his own, that we came together again. I made an extra effort to go home regularly, and the phone conversations that had always been with my mother were now directed to him. I watched him grieve, and I encouraged him to get out and socialize and meet new people. My brothers resented the fact that he started square dancing and dating so soon after Mom's death. I tried to be the buffer, which meant they then directed their disapproval at me. This only worsened after he met and married Ruth. My brothers thought the 1999 formal wedding and reception ridiculous, and they scoffed at the idea that Daddy had asked my husband Homer and me to be in the wedding party. A week after the wedding, having sold the home place, Daddy auctioned off almost everything and moved into her duplex, a decision of which my brothers totally disapproved. They rarely, if ever, visited him in his new home. I liked Ruth and was glad Daddy had found someone. Homer and I were a regular part of their lives for the next eleven years, either by phone or in person. For the most part, they lived happily and independently, and they would have gladly lived that way forever.

But time has a mind of its own and brings its inevitable, unwelcome changes. Ruth's death in October 2011 was not only the end of her life, but it also signaled the beginning of Daddy's Long Goodbye.

FIRST FALL AND WINTER

Daddy and the Westies, Winter 2012

The Decision

It was 2011, and my eighty-nine-year old father was dying of kidney failure. He had known it for a long time, but I had just learned of the seriousness of his condition the preceding fall. Suspecting there were things he wasn't telling me, I asked to join him on one of his doctor's appointments. "Sure," he said, "you'll like this guy." He was right. I liked the kidney specialist very much. But I didn't like the news at all. Daddy was in stage four of renal failure. He had been for some time, and the prognosis was bleak. "His body is operating on only one kidney," his doctor said, "and the functionality of that one is dwindling. Nothing can reverse this. At his age, a transplant is not an option. That leaves dialysis, and your father has said he doesn't want to do that. Have you changed your mind about that, LaVerne?"

"Nope," my father answered. "I ain't gonna spend the rest of my life hooked up to no machine. You gotta die some time. I'm gonna make the most of whatever time I got. No machine."

The doctor turned to me and said gently, "He's been adamant about that from the beginning. I can't say I blame him. It would prolong his life, but maybe only for six months. Dialysis can be pretty miserable. Every patient has to decide for himself." Then he directed my attention to the handful of test results he held. "These tests show the status of your dad's kidneys. The purpose of the kidneys is to filter toxins from the blood. Your dad's kidneys aren't doing that very well anymore. Eventually they will fail entirely, and that is what will cause his death."

"Daddy, do you understand that?" I asked.

"Yeah, I understand it," he grunted. "None of this is news to me."

"Well, I sure didn't know how serious this is," I responded. "Why didn't you tell me?"

"Didn't wanna worry you," he said. "You worry too much."

The doctor must have seen the stricken look on my face. "He's on top of this," he assured me. "He takes his meds. He comes to his appointments. We're doing the best we can, given the hand he was dealt."

Finally, I forced myself to ask the question. "How much time does he have?"

"Impossible to know for sure," the doctor said. "Given the pattern of decline he's in, and without dialysis, maybe six months to a year. But you just never know."

"Stop worryin' about it," Daddy said. "I ain't dead yet. Now let's get out of here."

I spent the next several months thinking about my dad's prognosis, mostly trying to assure myself that the doctor had it all wrong. My dad was still living independently, caring for Ruth, who had suffered a debilitating stroke some years before. He helped her in and out of her wheelchair, drove her to church and her appointments. His garden was the envy of the neighborhood, and although he used a cane if I nagged him about it, he got around pretty well for a guy with two hip replacements and a bum ankle. He was plagued with arthritis, but that had been the case as long as I could remember. He square danced for a couple hours every week, which is how he had met Ruth. He still climbed into a tree stand every November to deer hunt. He didn't suffer from incontinence or any of the other embarrassments of old age. Dying? I didn't think so. He was doing just fine.

But all that changed after Ruth was hospitalized with pneumonia in October, shortly after their eleventh anniversary. Prior to that, her children had already expressed concerns that Daddy was declining. He wasn't as strong as he used to be, and he was finding her care to be more and more difficult, they said. He was also having trouble driving after dark. When we gathered in her hospital room and her family suggested that the two of them move into assisted living, Daddy was livid. "I can take care of her, just like I always have!" he shouted. "We're staying right where we are!!"

The scene was ugly, and we were at an impasse, so a doctor came in to mediate. He quietly asked Ruth where she preferred to live, and if she thought her husband could take care of her. "He always has. I want to go home with him," she whispered as she squeezed his hand. "Well," the doctor said, "OK. But first you'll need to spend a little time in a nursing home to get your strength back. Is that all right?" Ruth and Daddy agreed to this compromise.

Ruth's family members clearly had their doubts, and so did I. Since I didn't see my dad daily, I thought they probably had a better handle on this than I did. But my dad was a stubborn guy. When he made up his mind about something, nobody could change it. Except maybe God. And that's what happened.

Ruth was moved from the hospital to a nursing home, but she died before she could return with Daddy to their house in Spencer. Daddy was heartbroken. He stayed outwardly strong throughout the funeral and the subsequent decision-making, but he was clearly depressed. Ruth's children, who owned the house in which he lived, said he was welcome to remain there indefinitely. They would continue to include him in their lives, they assured me. This was very important, because frankly, Ruth's family was much more involved with my dad than his own children and extended family. I called him regularly and visited once a month or so, but I lived a hundred miles to the north. My brother Ken lived a hundred miles to the south. Two of my other brothers had already died. And my brother Dale, who lived nearby, had never accepted Dad's decision to marry Ruth after Mom died, so he rarely stopped in to visit. The Noeldners, on the other hand, had embraced Daddy from the beginning. They had frequent family gatherings and dinners to which Dad was always invited, and they routinely dropped in at the house. But, I suspected that would change when their mother was no longer a regular presence in their lives.

After Ruth's death, Daddy was lost. He went through the motions of everyday life, but he wasn't eating much and was losing weight. I rarely saw his impish grin or heard him laugh. As we headed into winter, I wondered how he would ever manage alone.

In the past, Homer and I had discussed the possibility of Daddy living with us someday. Homer had been open to the idea, but since this was merely speculative and in the distant future, we never really explored it. Homer and my dad had always seen eye to eye and had similar interests. Now it seemed time to return to this discussion.

But before we made any decisions, I wanted to see Dad's doctor again. It had been three months since the last appointment. The doctor expressed his condolences to my dad the minute he walked in, and said, "How are you doing, LaVerne? Not so good, I'm thinking, based on these numbers." He'd lost ten pounds, his creatinine levels were higher, and in general he was declining. "Why are you losing all this weight?' the doctor asked.

"Don't know," Daddy said. "Just not hungry, I guess. Nobody to cook for either."

"Maybe you need someone to cook for you," the doctor suggested.

That was my opening. "I've been thinking about that," I said. "I'm worried that he's not taking care of himself. I'm worried that he won't be able to live alone much longer. I'm worried that as his health declines, he's going to need more care."

"You worry too much," Dad said.

I turned back to the doctor for support. "As his kidneys continue to fail, what's going to happen?"

The doctor took a deep breath, then began. "It is a gradual process. As the levels of waste begin to build up in his blood, he will have less and less energy, and less and less appetite. He will sleep more and more, until he's sleeping nearly all the time. He will become less responsive, drifting in and out of consciousness. He will be heavily medicated for pain, so he won't suffer much. But eventually his system will shut completely down. I know this is hard to hear, but as deaths go, it's a gentle one." The silence hung in the room.

"He's going to need a caregiver by then, isn't he?" I asked. "He can't possibly go through this living alone, right?"

"Right," the doctor said. He turned to Dad. "I know you don't want to hear this, LaVerne, but you've got some decisions to make pretty soon."

"Could be," Daddy said, "but not today. Let's go, Kid."

When I got home, I shared the discussion with Homer. I asked him how he felt about Daddy living with us, given this scenario. We'd be assuming the burden for his care for the next six months to a year if the doctor's timeline was accurate. The alternative was overseeing his life in assisted living. We both knew that because my dad and I were particularly close, it would fall to me to see him through this. Since I had recently semi-retired, I had the time to devote to him. I told Homer I wasn't sure what Dad would want to do, but if we were going to offer to open our home to him, we'd better be sure that we were willing to follow through. After mulling it over for a few days, Homer said, "Call him and invite him to live with us."

"Are you sure?" I asked.

"Are you?" he countered.

"No," I admitted, "but it feels like the right thing to do."

I made the phone call. I opened with, "Hey, Daddy. How you doin'?"

"OK, I guess," he said.

"No, I don't think so, Daddy. I don't think you're OK at all," I countered. It was now or never, so I plunged ahead. "I don't think you can be on your own too much longer. Homer and I talked about it, and we think you should come live with us. And if you don't want to do that, then we need to find you an assisted living apartment either in Marshfield or Rhinelander. Don't even think about the money, because you can afford it, and you know it. You need somebody to keep an eye on you, cook for you, run you to appointments, keep you company. It's not good for you to be alone all the time."

He was quiet for a long time. Then he said, "Could be you're right. I'll think about it."

I called my brothers and told them about Daddy's medical prognosis, my offer for him to live with us or help him find assisted living, and that Dad was considering it. I got a "whatever he wants to do" sort of response and no offer of assistance. I didn't really expect one.

Several weeks passed as we waited for Daddy's decision. Homer was busily converting what had been a bonus room above our garage into a bedroom for us; if Dad moved in, he could have our room next to the bathroom on the main floor. I was excited that there was impetus to finish the room. We had wanted to do it eventually, and as Homer hammered away, it became more and more beautiful and inviting. Even if Daddy didn't move in, we'd have a new master bedroom and half bath.

In December Daddy reluctantly made his decision. If it was a choice between assisted living and us, he'd move to our home in Rhinelander. Except for his stint in the Army, he'd lived in Central Wisconsin his whole life. He had gone to school there, farmed there, raised his kids there, attended church there, and most of his family and friends were still there. He might as well be moving to Siberia as far as he was concerned. But when it came down to a choice between the devil he knew and the devil he didn't know, we appeared the lesser of two evils.

The Transition

We notified my brothers that he would be moving north with us at the end of January 2012. Dale's wife, Rosann, was sympathetic, supportive, and appreciative. Dale said little or nothing, nor did Ken. This was up to us, seemed to be the unspoken message, and if we thought it was a good idea, then it was fine by them. I don't know that any of us thought it was a *good* idea. It just seemed like the path of least resistance.

I started moving carloads of Daddy's stuff north between my consulting gigs in December. I was working with several project-based charter schools around the state, and on my way home, I sometimes stopped at Dad's. I arrived one Friday night not too long before Christmas to find probably twenty large boxes of assorted chocolates neatly stacked on his kitchen table. These were his customary Christmas gifts to children, grandchildren, and in-laws. "The wrapping paper's in the basement," he said.

"Realllly?" I said, drawing the word out as long as possible. "You should probably go get it and get these wrapped."

"No," he said with a grin. "That's your job. I've been waiting for you to show up. You wrap; I'll write out the tags."

And in that moment a subtle, but enormous, shift of

power occurred. Daddy had handed over his responsibilities for everyday duties to me. At the time it seemed harmless and charming and sweet. I had no way of anticipating how heavy that weight would eventually become.

Before leaving to head home again that weekend, Dad directed me to load my car with items he wanted to take north. He knew he wouldn't need them for the next month or so, and it seemed a waste for me to drive an empty car home. He still didn't want to leave the lovely home he had shared with Ruth, but by this time he was resigned to the move. I think hardest for him was abandoning her many possessions that had surrounded the two of them for eleven years in this house. Leaving the many pieces of his wife behind was like losing her all over again. The only thing he took that wasn't his was an old chipped ceramic rabbit that had guarded their front door from the time he had married her. "Take that," he said. "I don't think anyone else wants it. Ruth made it in ceramics class." I crammed it into the backseat of my car, thinking, "I guess this ugly thing is going to sit in front of my house now. Geez." But before I could even close the door, it tumbled to the curb, smashing into a billion pieces. Daddy didn't say anything. He didn't have to. His face said everything. "Oh, I'm so sorry," I lamented. "Maybe we can glue it back together."

"Forget it," he said. "It'll never work. Everything breaks eventually." And I knew he was talking about a whole lot more than lawn ornaments.

I don't have many regrets regarding my dad. I did the best I could, but breaking that rabbit was a sign that I would fall short, despite my best efforts. Life is fragile and everything does break, sooner or later. As I waved goodbye that morning and eased my Jeep away from the curb, I promised myself I would take better care of him than I did that bunny. I would be gentle, and I would be careful. And maybe that would be good enough.

The Drive

There is nothing quite as cold as a Wisconsin January. That night was no exception. The temperature was in the single digits, the wind was howling, and the snow blew across the road in white gusts of loneliness. It was already dark at five p.m. as I followed Homer's tail lights north. His pickup was crammed past capacity with my father's belongings, tarps and bungee cords attempting to hold everything in place as the wind offered its steady resistance. "*The Beverly Hillbillies*," I thought. "My life has become the opening of *The Beverly Hillbillies*."

Crowded into his Toyota jammed with the rest of his possessions, my father huddled against the cold. I could see him hunched inside his jacket, shivering despite the blasting heater. His handsome old face was without expression, and he wasn't saying much. He never did. "Are you cold, Daddy?" I asked. "I'm always cold," he answered. We would repeat that exchange countless times in the coming months.

I also noticed that he smelled funny. Not like body odor. Not like dirty clothes, or urine, or feces. Just...odd. Not overwhelming, but unpleasant. I blamed it on the cramped quarters and the stale air. Later, when I mentioned it to Homer, he said, "I think it's the kidney failure. I think it comes from the toxins his body is building up. I've noticed it before." This was the first time I had noticed it, and it troubled me, so I tried to push it to the back of my mind as I thought back to earlier in the day.

Mid-afternoon we had loaded up the last of his possessions. Dale and his two sons assisted at my request, but they didn't offer to follow us north to Rhinelander to help us get Dad settled in. They simply jumped into their own vehicles and sped off, leaving us alone to contend with the rest of the journey. It didn't bother me at the time, but it did later when I realized how angry Homer was that they weren't assuming more responsibility for Daddy's move. He and I were the ones who arrived home tired and hungry and cold after the drive north, still having to carry everything into our house to get Dad settled, while they had been home for hours watching TV and drinking beer. Like many other examples of lack of forethought, I should have anticipated this and asked them to help. They would have. They might not have liked it, but it would have been the right thing to do. And it might have forestalled some of the resentment that began to grow in Homer that very night.

Thinking back on it now, there were a lot of things we should have done differently. Just as Homer and I didn't lay out our expectations to my brothers, we didn't lay them out to Daddy, and we didn't lay them out to each other. We innocently believed that there wouldn't be any issues, or that everything would just work itself out. We hadn't talked about the daily schedule, about laundry, groceries, rent, meals, expenses, driving—not any of the mundane decisions that people who share a household should talk about before ever moving in together. I didn't even think about it. I was so busy trying to make the transition easy that I didn't do anything to prepare for the long-term living arrangements. I was finally thinking about all this as we drove on into the night, but how could I bring it up now? There was no turning back, and it seemed pointless. But then I remembered the few months when Grandpa Hugo had lived on the farm with us. He was my dad's father, widowed, and what seemed then a thousand years old. It had been a horrible experience. Grandpa's residence with us was disastrous, dividing Daddy and Mom, us kids, and ultimately Grandpa and Daddy. By the time he moved out, the relationships were damaged beyond repair.

I was remembering that as I looked at my dad. He was about the age that Grandpa had been when he had moved in with us. "Dad," I began. "I don't know how this living together thing is going to work out. I think it will be OK, but I don't know. Now, you never say much, but if things come up that we need to talk about, you have to tell us. And we have to tell you. Because I love you, and I don't want anything to ever change the way you and I feel about each other. You know?"

"Oh, you worry too much," he laughed. "Everything will be fine."

"Well, I hope so," I said. "But I've been thinking about what a mess it became when Grandpa lived with us. I couldn't stand it if things turned out like that."

There was a long pause. Then Daddy said, "But he was an asshole."

"Uh, yeah," I said, "but maybe that relationship wouldn't have gone south, if you and Mom had tried to talk to him more about things that were going wrong."

"There was no talking to him," Daddy said.

"Still," I persisted, "you have to promise me that we're going to talk about issues as they come up, before they get to be a big deal. Because if it comes down to your having to move somewhere else to avoid us having a falling out, that's what I want to do. I don't ever want to lose the relationship we have right now. Do you promise?"

"OK, Kid, if that's what it takes to make you feel better. But you worry too much."

I felt a little better. But I never stopped worrying.

Going to the Dogs

It was a long, cold trip north. We drove until the wind loosened the tarps on Homer's pickup to the point where he had to pull over on the freeway to reattach them. He was struggling with them in the sub-zero temps when the state trooper pulled in behind him. He got the usual safety lecture and not much assistance, but, thankfully, no ticket either. Homer was in a foul mood by the time we finally pulled in the driveway. All three of us were exhausted, and we dreaded the task of unloading all Dad's stuff and dragging it into his bedroom. I said maybe it could wait until morning, but Homer said, "Might as well get it done now."

When we walked in the door, the dogs were as usual delighted to see us. The two Westies, Lily and Daisy, and Riley, our Akita, circled around our legs, barking a merry hello and sniffing the intruder. My dad had always loved dogs, and he was happy to see the Westies. On the other hand, he was not so crazy about Riley. Dad settled into his recliner, the Westies jumped on his lap, and from that perch he supervised while Homer and I moved his stuff in. It was several hours later when we finally staggered in with the last of it, and well past Daddy's regular bedtime.

He was already dozing in the chair. We started to clear off his bed so he could finally settle in. "Don't you want to take a bath first, LaVerne?" Homer asked, rather pointedly, I thought.

"Nope," Dad said. "I take my bath on Saturday."

"Well, after the long trip up here, you might sleep better after you've had a bath," Homer began again.

"Saturday," Dad said.

"Suit yourself," Homer said.

We retreated to the living room while Dad rummaged around in his closet. "Never noticed before how much noise those closet doors make," Homer observed. "And why doesn't he want to take a bath? He stinks."

"He's tired," I defended. "We all are. Let's just get some rest."

"You know," Homer said, "we wouldn't be this tired if we'd had some more help. Dale should have come up here with us. It's his dad—not mine."

"I didn't ask him to," I responded. "And keep your voice down. If you want to be mad at somebody about tonight, be mad at me. I'm going to bed. Where are my girls?" I said. "Gotta have my girls sleeping with us."

"Last I saw they were with your dad," Homer said. "At least maybe we'll have the whole bed to ourselves for a change. He might like their company. They were used to sleeping in there with us, you know. If we're lucky, maybe they'll decide to stay with him."

"That would be awful for you," I kidded. "I guess we'll let them decide."

It was nearly midnight by the time we crawled into bed. I fell into a sound sleep almost immediately but woke up around two to an eerie, otherworldly howling.

Homer was already on his feet. "What the hell?" he muttered.

"Coyotes?" I asked.

"I don't know," he said. "I think it's one of the girls. Sounds like she's in distress. We better go find her."

Homer rushed downstairs and outside, dreading the possible carnage. Even with a fenced-in yard, coyotes and wolves are a menace to dogs in northern Wisconsin. And we had seen and heard plenty of them in our neighborhood.

Meanwhile, I searched the basement. The pitiful howling and crying continued, and I moved from room to room, closet to closet in search. Nothing. I could still hear one of the dogs. I went back upstairs, looked in the hall closet, the bathroom. Nothing. Then I looked at the closed door to Daddy's bedroom. No way, I thought. Way, the other voice in my head responded. I knocked on the door. "Daddy?"

Nothing. I pushed the bedroom door open, and there was Daisy, jumping up and down with delight to see me at two in the morning. "Where's your sister?" I whispered.

The whimpering seemed to get louder. I opened the accordion doors to the closet, and Lily came bounding out in a rush of relief.

Homer came crashing in behind me. "Where the hell was she?" he demanded.

"Inside the closet," I said. "She probably went in when Dad was hanging up his clothes, and he didn't know she was in there. I bet she fell asleep and woke up in the middle of the night wondering where she was, wanted out, and started howling."

"Well, why the hell didn't he let her out?" Homer said incredulously.

"Because he didn't hear her," I whispered, unnecessarily it seemed. "He's still asleep. He didn't even hear me knock on the door. Let's get out of here before we wake him up."

"Yeah," Homer replied dryly. "Wouldn't want to wake the ol' boy up at this hour. Come on, Littles," he said to the Westies. "You two better get used to sleeping upstairs."

The four of us tromped back up the stairs and settled into our king size bed.

It was clear that life had changed, in big and little ways. And this was just the beginning.

Learning to Dance

My dad was up at eight the next morning. We were not. It had been a short night, and as was often the case, Homer and I planned to sleep in. But I could hear Daddy moving around downstairs, and since I still thought of him as a guest rather than a resident, I got up, dressed, and joined him downstairs while Homer and the girls continued to snore. The last time I had been at his house, Daddy had told me to rustle up whatever I wanted to eat. "I ain't no short order cook," he had said. I thought I would try the same approach.

"What do you want for breakfast, Dad? There's cereal, bread for toast, eggs, bacon, juice, milk...just help yourself to whatever you want when you're ready."

"Well, I gotta take my medicine," Dad said, "and I have to eat something first. I'll just have whatever you're having."

Since Homer and I usually had a late brunch on the weekend, often after eleven or noon, I knew this wasn't an option. Oh well, I thought. It's just the first day. I poured his cereal, toasted the bread, buttered it, served him some juice and milk, and did the same for myself. Not exactly the omelet or waffles I'd been looking forward to all week, but it was breakfast nonetheless. Daddy finished his meal in silence, carried his dishes to the dishwasher, loaded it, and settled into his recliner. I suggested he go through his Army footlocker and sort out what he wanted to display and what he wanted to keep in storage. He reached in and removed the box of letters and cards he and Ruth had received on their wedding day, along with subsequent cards for all occasions over the last eleven years. His old hands carefully opened them up, one by one, as he worked his way through the stack. Once in a while he'd hand me a framed picture or knickknack he wanted to have in his room, but mostly he just silently traveled that road of reminiscence. Finally, he finished, put the pieces of his past back into the trunk, and said, "Is there room for this at the foot of my bed? I'd kinda like to have it where I can get at it."

"Sure," I said, and dragged the beat-up old footlocker to its next utilitarian location.

"Look what else I found," he said when I walked back into the living room. "Recognize this?" he grinned.

It was a copy of *Conversations with My Mother*, the memoir I'd written after Mom's death. It was a record of the journey from the night she died through the five subsequent years of adjustment our family experienced. I'd given preliminary copies to everyone in the family at Christmas in 2003 so they'd know what I was publishing. No one said much of anything at the time. I think Ken was the only one who thought it was a fair treatment of the events we'd gone through, but I self-published it anyway. Here it was now, in Daddy's gnarled old hands. "Think I'm going to read this again," Daddy said. "It'll give me somethin' to do." With that, he opened the cover and settled in to read, enveloped head to feet in two afghans. He was still reading when Homer staggered out of bed several hours later.

By then it was time for Homer's breakfast, and Dad's

lunch. Daddy was famous for three square meals a day no matter how old he was. And he expected them to be at the same time every day—since retirement, at eight, noon, and six. Homer and I usually just ate twice a day, and sometimes only once. Lunch was not at all a part of our routine—mainly due to the late breakfasts. Dinner waited until Homer got home from logging, and he typically worked until dark, unless rain or snow intervened. We might eat any time between six and nine thirty, depending on the season and the weather. This was not something I had thought much about when contemplating Dad's moving in. Clearly, we were all going to need to make some adjustments to our daily schedule. Our dance of compromise began then, with my making omelets for everybody after what seemed to me just four short hours since I had served Dad his breakfast.

I was cleaning up dishes for a second time, when Homer said, "So what are we going to have for supper tonight?"

Supper??? We'd had breakfast, we'd had lunch, and we were going to have supper too? Of course, we were. That's what normal families did. It's just that after thirty years together, we had never been normal, and we'd really never even been a family. A sudden, obvious realization settled heavily on my shoulders. It was this: whether minuet or waltz, polka or tango, dances are meant for two, not three. This new living arrangement was going to require considerable finesse and practice to avoid stepping on toes. I sighed and headed downstairs to the freezer looking for inspiration and an answer to a much bigger issue than the evening's menu.

"And hey, while you're down there," Homer hollered after me, "bring up some apples. Your dad and I could go for a pie." And with that, we once again, switched partners.

No More Driving

Shortly after Daddy moved in, the appointments and trips to town began. Our house is about twenty minutes from everywhere, along winding roads built between lakes and creeks. The first time Daddy and I headed for Rhinelander to pick up meds and groceries, Dad said we should take his car, since many of the chores were related to him. I said sure, got in the passenger side, and waited for him to join me. He came around to my door, opened it, and said, "No, you drive. I don't know where I'm going. I'll just get us lost."

I countered, "I think you should drive. It will help you to learn your way around. I never pay attention to where I'm going when I'm the passenger, but I have to when I'm the driver. Driving will get your more familiar with the area."

"Nope," Dad said. "You're going with me; you might as well drive."

"Well," I compromised. "Let's get you familiar with the area, and then the next time you can drive."

He said nothing, just jerked his head in the direction of the driver's seat and got in beside me.

As I drove, I pointed out the landmarks and road names, indicating turns along the way. I took the same route to and from town, although there are several other choices. When we returned home and I parked his car in our driveway, I said, "Well, think you'll remember that?"

"Nope," he said. "I never see roads that wind around like this. You oughta call it Snake Road, not Pine Lake Road."

I laughed and said, "I suppose it's pretty different from the flat farm country you're used to driving in. You'll get the hang of it." Again, he replied by saying nothing.

Subsequent drives elicited the same response. Finally, I said, "You know, Dad, I think it's important that you're comfortable driving yourself where you want to go. There's a senior citizen center in town, meals for the elderly at the town hall, all kinds of stuff you might want to do, and I'm not always going to be able to drive you. When I'm off doing my consulting work and Homer's logging, we don't want you stranded here unable to go anywhere."

"I got no place I have to be," Daddy said. "I can't see as well as I used to, and I don't know my way around. I can wait for you to take me places when you're home. That's good enough."

"But you don't want to lose your independence like that, do you?" I challenged.

"Kid," he said, "I already lost my independence when I moved here. Driving don't change that."

"Well, maybe not for him," Homer sputtered when I announced Dad's decision, "but what about us? He's perfectly capable of driving himself around. Why should we have to do it for him? You mean every time he wants to go somewhere, we have to drop everything and take him?"

"Homer," I said gently. "Maybe this is a blessing in disguise. You've seen him drive. You know how terrible he was even when he was younger and could see. It's even worse now. This way he stops driving before he hurts himself or someone else, and we don't have to be the bad guys who take his keys away from him. Let this happen."

"Ridiculous," Homer maintained. "It's not that tough to drive here. Rhinelander's half the size of Marshfield, and he can learn the roads. If he won't drive himself, we're going to have to haul him everywhere."

"That's going to happen sooner or later, anyway," I reminded him. "For a year we can manage this. And, by the way, do you remember the trip you guys took thirty years ago out West when you shared the driving?"

"Jesus Christ," Homer said. "How could I forget? He took over the driving, I fell asleep, and the next thing I knew I woke up and he was headed the wrong way down the interstate driving seventy-five miles per hour. I don't know how we didn't end up being killed that night. I still don't know what the hell he was thinking."

"Well, it's worse now," I said. "If he wants us to drive, we're going to. We'll use his car for his errands and let him pay for gas, but we'll drive. I don't want to argue about this anymore."

Homer made several attempts on future trips to cajole my dad into driving, but Dad always politely but steadfastly refused. "I'm done with that," he said, and he was as good as his word. Homer and I–mostly I–became his chauffeurs. He always gave me plenty of advance notice about appointments that needed to be kept and errands he wanted to run, and for the most part it wasn't much of a problem. But he never went anywhere alone after that. The man who had run his own household and cared for his invalid wife had assumed the role of a dependent, albeit patient and appreciative, child.

Second Opinion

Once Daddy moved in, I had a long list of caregiver responsibilities to set in motion. The first was to get referrals from his previous doctors in Marshfield for new physicians in our area. Fortunately, the Marshfield Clinic has a satellite clinic in Woodruff, so this process was relatively easy, despite needing to find an internal medicine doctor who specialized in geriatrics, an ophthalmologist to deal with advancing glaucoma, and a renal specialist. Dad also needed to change VA clinics and doctors. All the prescriptions for the many meds Dad was taking had to be transferred as well. The first couple of months were a flurry of thirty-five-mile one-way drives to meet and greet his new medical team. I was doing consultant work part-time in the southern part of the state, so it was Homer who drove Daddy to meet his new nephrologist. I desperately wanted to be there since so much of my father's care would be in his hands, but circumstances prevented me from attending.

Homer's report from the new doctor was pretty dismal. I had somehow hoped that perhaps a second opinion would provide a cheerier prognosis, but it was not to be. Dad's levels were worse than they had been at his last appointment in Marshfield. He'd lost more weight, he was fatigued, and he appeared to be spiraling downward. His new doctor, a charming fellow with a great bedside manner and a quick wit, easily established a rapport with Dad. When he raised the dialysis question, Dad was adamant that it wasn't an option. Dr. Flannigan nodded and said, "I don't blame you. It can be pretty unpleasant." Homer asked Flannigan to project what kind of time Dad had left, with and without dialysis.

"Hard to say for sure," Flannigan said. "At his current rate of decline, he probably has six months without dialysis, a year if he opts for it. But we never know."

"A year if I'm hooked up to a machine?" Dad repeated. "That ain't livin'. I'll take the six months. A man's gotta die sometime."

"Well," Flannigan said, "that's your call, and you've obviously thought about it. But in the meantime, we're going to do what we can to make you comfortable, see if we can increase your energy, and get you to gain some weight. We can't cure you, but maybe we can slow this decline down some and make you feel a little better. No guarantees, though."

"There ain't never no guarantees," Daddy said.

"No there ain't," Flannigan agreed with a wink. "I'll see you in a month."

I was crying by the time Homer finished telling the story. "Why are you so upset?" he asked. "None of this is news, right? You already heard all this in Marshfield."

"I know," I said, "but somehow I hoped things would get better."

"You're a smart woman," Homer gently admonished. "You know that's not going to happen. All you can do is take it one day at a time. Just like him."

"Well, in the meantime, I think I'll try to see what kind of help is out there for senior citizens and their caregivers," I said. "We're going to need some help sooner or later."

I reached for my *Senior Citizens Resource Guide* and a pen and paper to start another to-do list.

Asking for Help

For most of my life I have not been very good at asking for help. I have always figured that I can do everything on my own, and even when I can't, no one else should be expected to shoulder my burdens. However, I also have been a firm believer that knowledge is power. I knew from friends whose own parents were aging that resources were available, and that the Oneida County Center on Aging was a good place to start. Dad didn't think we really needed to get any information, but after I made an appointment for the two of us with one of their intake workers, he agreed to go with me.

The social worker was lovely. She ushered us in, covertly watched as Dad hobbled in without his cane, and offered us seats. She introduced herself and asked how she could help. I explained that Dad had recently moved in with us, what his medical prognosis was, and the timetable the doctor had projected. I told her we didn't need anything yet, but I wanted to be ready when we did. She handed us a folder full of brochures describing various services available to seniors, including activities at the Senior Citizen Center, meals on wheels, drivers, medical equipment, medical alert systems, in-home care, and hospice. I told her I never knew there was so much help out there. She affirmed that most people didn't, and it really was a shame. She took my phone number and said she would touch base in a month to see how we were doing, but that I was welcome to call any time with questions. Then she asked Daddy if there was anything she could help him with, and he pointed his arthritic thumb at me said, "Nope. I don't need no help as long as I got her."

"Well, then, LaVerne," she said, "you're a lucky man. But here's my card in case things change."

He handed it to me with a smile, and said, "She'll probably need this more than I will." And as always, he was right.

The Schedule

Daddy was a man of routine. When he was farming, he got up every morning at 6 a.m. and ate two strips of bacon, two fried eggs, two pieces of toast, and a cup of coffee. Then he went to the barn for the morning milking. He returned to the house and had his second breakfast of a bowl of cereal three hours later. By noon he was ready for lunch. He expected it ready and on the table no later than 12:15. Mom served supper at 6, and by 6:30 Dad was back in the barn for evening chores. By 9 he'd finished milking and was in the house, watching TV while eating a bowl of ice cream or popcorn. He was in bed as soon as he finished watching the weather on the local news, then up the following day to begin the cycle all over again. Any deviation from this schedule made him irritable. He rarely complained if his routine was undisturbed, but if a meal was a half an hour late, he'd claim he already had a headache. "Hangry" was a word they could have coined to describe my father any time a meal was delayed. After he retired from farming, he continued to get up at the same time every morning, go to bed at the same time every night, and eat three square meals a day with an evening snack. He did forgo the second breakfast since he wasn't burning as many calories as he used to. As he aged, he had to take more and more meds with food, so he became even more rigid about mealtimes. Since he was always active and had a speedy metabolism, he never had to worry about his weight. It was three meals a day, every day, every week, every month, every year for ninety years. And then he moved in with us...

My routine was much like my father's until I retired. During the week I was up at 6, showered, dressed, breakfasted, and at school by 7:15, home again by 5:30, ready for dinner at 6, and always in bed by 10, sometimes by 8. Teaching was exhausting, and unless I got plenty of sleep, I'd get sick. I lived for sleeping in on weekends. During the week, with only twenty minutes for lunch, I usually skipped it or had a soda, so I became used to two meals a day.

Homer was running his own business, and his schedule was crazy. For many years as he was getting established, he worked eighteen-hour days, six or seven days a week. Meals and bedtimes were erratic to say the least. He usually was on the road by 4 a.m. while I was still sleeping, so he rustled up his own breakfast. He grabbed a candy bar or two for lunch, guzzled Mountain Dew when he couldn't stay awake anymore, and when he finally arrived home at 10 or 11, I not only had already eaten my dinner hours before, but I was often sound asleep. He'd open a can of something, heat it up, stay awake long enough to eat it, climb into the shower and then stagger to bed. It was hard on him and our marriage, but he was young and ambitious, and we survived. Years later he slowed down to only ten-hour work days, then to eight. Even at that, his schedule rarely mirrored mine. He typically worked until it was too dark to see, arrived home several hours after me, and stayed up until midnight or one in the morning. He'd get up around 8 or 9, and by then I'd already been at work a couple of hours. All those long days in previous years soured him forever on early rising. In short, our schedules were rarely the same, except on weekends when we'd both sleep in, have brunch around 11, and eat together in the evening whenever we both got hungry again.

I hadn't thought about any of that when we decided to invite Daddy to live with us. But it became very clear very early on that something was going to have to change if we were all going to be able to coexist in the same house. When I look back on it now, it's surprising that Dad was the one who changed his habits to accommodate ours. He started staying up until 10 at night, rather than retiring at 9. He'd remain in bed until 9 in the morning, rather than his usual 7 a.m. rising. I tried to have a substantial breakfast ready for all of us by 10 or 10:30, and he got in the habit of having an afternoon snack rather than lunch. Homer made an effort to come home earlier, so we could eat dinner between 6 and 7. I'm sure it wasn't ideal from my dad's point of view, but he liked my cooking, and I spoiled him with lots of desserts that he hadn't been getting when he lived alone, and he adjusted. It was only when I was off on my consulting gigs, and he was reduced to Homer's dinners of beans or Spam, that he was unhappy, but even then, he didn't complain, just ate an extra piece of bread and butter rather than the "main course."

Homer always had a ready supply of chocolate on hand as well, and Dad enjoyed that when it was offered, but he never asked for it. He never asked for anything, and he never scoured the cupboards or the fridge for snacks of any kind. Sometimes I wish that he had, so it would feel as if he was more like family, less like a guest. He liked being waited on, and he came to expect it, even though he never actually voiced that attitude. Still, he made his own bed, cleared his place at the table, and gradually adapted to a "schedule" that would have infuriated him when he was younger. The three of us each compromised in a way that everyone could live with, and we settled into a new less-than-routine "routine."

Always on Sunday

"There's just one thing I ask," Daddy said before he moved in. "I need to find a church to go to on Sundays. Can you help me with that?"

"Yeah," I said, "I may be a heathen, but I know where all the churches are in town. I'll fix you up."

I smiled to myself. Apparently, Daddy intended to keep the promise he had made to Ruth twelve years earlier. My father had been baptized and confirmed at Immanuel Lutheran Church in Marshfield. He was a lifelong member, and my mom's funeral was held there too, but he had never been a regular-church goer. When he was farming, there was never time to get there, and after he retired, he continued to enjoy Sunday mornings in his Lazy Boy. Until he met Ruth. She was also a Lutheran, but a much more committed one than Daddy. Regular church attendance was a way of life for her and her children. One of her sons was a Lutheran minister, and it was he who officiated at their wedding service when Dad finally won her over. She had resisted his early discussions of marriage, but he was persistent, and she finally succumbed with the caveat, "If you marry me, you marry my church." He agreed, and he was as good as his word. Every Sunday they drove to the church in Loyal where they had been married. My father became a regular fixture there along with her, and he enjoyed a new fellowship of faith. Ruth and her kids prayed before meals and at bedtime, and Daddy easily adapted to those habits which had never been a part of his life with Mom. After Ruth's stroke, Daddy continued to drive the two of them to church every Sunday until she was hospitalized. When she died, I sat beside him in the front pew at her funeral, and I wondered if that would be the last time he attended a service there. But no. Daddy kept his promise. He continued to attend services in Loyal until he moved north. Prior to doing that, he shared with me his intention to regularly attend church, and now it was time to help him find a new place to worship.

I hadn't been a practicing Lutheran since my brother Cliff's funeral. There, next to my grieving parents, brothers, and Cliff's children, I listened in disbelief when the minister mentioned as if in passing, "Perhaps the series of deaths this family has experienced in recent months is a gentle reminder by God of the need for regular church attendance. While God does not punish, it is true that the Machtan family rarely attends Sunday services, except at Christmas and Easter, and God clearly would like their presence throughout the year."

"You son of a bitch," I thought. "My twenty-one-year-old brother was just killed in a car crash, leaving behind a widow, two children, and one on the way, and this is your idea of comfort?? How dare you? What sort of message of solace and love is this? I'm done here."

When the service ended, I walked out of the church, and I did not return until my mother's funeral seventeen years later. It was equally depressing and joyless. The minister knew so little about my mother that he had to read her newspaper obituary to have enough to say. She deserved so much more, and that only served to reinforce my disillusionment with religion in general and the Missouri (Misery) Synod specifically. I have always believed in a higher power, but that deity had nothing to do with a clerical collar and stained glass.

Regardless of my lack of enthusiasm for Sunday services, I was determined to accommodate my dad's wishes. I told him that there were four Lutheran churches in Rhinelander, three of them within a three-block area. We'd start at the north end and work our way down until we found one that he liked. That first Sunday in January, he bathed the night before, got up early, dressed in his suit, and after breakfast we headed to the first of our church "auditions." I knew the minister of this particular church, which was coincidentally also named Immanuel. I had had Pastor Norm's children in class, attended weddings he had officiated, and had heard him speak several times. I liked him, so this seemed like a good place to start.

We were warmly welcomed by the ushers when we entered. Before the service officially began, Pastor Norm left the pulpit, walked to where his congregants were seated, and made several informal announcements about upcoming events and the status of ailing members for whom he asked for continued prayers, visits, cards, and phone calls. When he finished, he said, "Now let's rise and greet one another." The entire congregation stood as one, and not only did they say hello to the people next to them, they left their pews, moved up and down the center aisle, shaking hands, hugging, smiling, and saying good morning. "What the heck is this madness?" I wondered. This was the first of many wonderful differences I was about to experience in an Evangelical Lutheran Church of America. I hadn't realized that the church Dad and Ruth attended was also part of the ELCA, and that Dad was used to a very different style of worship from the one I had experienced as a kid. As the service continued, I discovered the hymns were lively and pretty, and I was actually moving to the beat. The accompaniment was as often on piano as the organ, and even the organ didn't sound as dirge-like as I remembered. A member of the congregation–a *woman*!!!!–read the two scripture lessons. The sermon was down-to-earth and human, and the message was all about love and service to others. Everything was connected to everyday life, and there were moments when Pastor Norm actually made me laugh out loud. The choir sang, standing in front of the church, beaming as they harmonized with sheer joy and enthusiasm for their message. Before communion, Pastor Norm asked us to share a sign of peace, something I had only ever seen before in Catholic churches. And most amazing of all, *everyone* was invited to participate in communion, regardless of religious affiliation. Every other church I'd ever been in required you to be a member of their exclusive elite to be part of this fundamental Christian ritual. As we filed out and shook Pastor Norm's hand, I told him we had enjoyed the service, and he said, "This wasn't really typical, what with the choir singing and all. That only happens maybe once a month. Why don't you come back next week to see what things are normally like?"

The following Sunday found us back at Immanuel. "What the heck?" I asked Dad, gesturing to a contemporary band set up to the right of the altar. Two acoustic guitars. Bass guitar. Piano. Hand drums. Flutes. Speakers. Monitors. Microphones. "Looks like we're gonna have a little music," Daddy said with a grin.

"But it's not an *organ*," I said. "It's not even just a piano. It's practically a full-fledged rock band! In a *Lutheran* church??????"

"Guess so," he said as he turned matter-of-factly to his bulletin.

That service was magical, start to finish. The Kyrie was so upbeat and happy. "Glory to God, Glory to God, and peace to God's people on earth," we sang as the drummer pounded out the rhythm and the rest of the musicians rocked the church with a message of love that practically had me dancing. The prelude. The Kyrie. The alleluia. The hymn of the day. A sung group prayer response of "Lord, listen to your children praying," accompanied by a gentle background guitar. Three communion songs. The sending song. And finally, the postlude. I wasn't ready to leave when the usher approached our pew. Such music! Such joy! And such a departure from the dour hymns that endlessly droned on the organ when I was a kid. A lot had changed in the past thirty-five years while I had been avoiding church. At least at this one.

As we filed out and I shook Pastor Norm's hand, I thanked him for a wonderful service. "Well, this wasn't really typical," Pastor Norm said, "what with the band playing and all. They don't usually do that."

"How often do they play?" I asked.

"Oh, about once a month," Norm said.

"Once a month?!?!" I thought. "Hot damn!!"

But this wasn't about me. This was about Dad. "Did you enjoy the music?" Norm asked Dad.

"It was real nice," Daddy said.

"Well, you should probably come back next week," Norm assured him, "to see what a regular service is like."

The following Sunday we were back in our pew, already creatures of habit. This time there was no choir and no band, but there was a children's sermon. Pastor Norm called all the littles of the church forward. He sat down on one of the steps that leads to the altar, surrounded by children who came skipping up the aisle, and delivered a special simplified version of the sermon's message just for them. After a brief prayer he sent them on their way, scrambling back to their parents waiting in the pews. Later in the service he invited them all back to the front of the church to witness a baptism. They sat on the steps and watched as an infant became the newest member of the church. When the baptism was finished, Pastor Norm gave the children seashells to take home, a reminder of their own baptisms. Their faces were filled with delight as they clutched their shells and applauded along with everyone else as the baby was presented as the newest member of the congregation. Then they skipped back to their seats and the service continued. When it was time for communion, the children were back at the rail with their parents, observing the distribution of bread and wine for which they would one day be old enough. In the meantime, they received a special blessing. "You are a child of God, and Jesus loves you, and you are blessed." Very simple and memorable.

"These children are full participants of this congregation," I marveled. "They're *not* to be seen and not heard. They aren't segregated from the rest of the congregation in Sunday school classes during the service. Faith Explorer classes are held between services so the kids can better understand what's going on. They obviously love Pastor Norm and, as unbelievable as it is, they seem to actually *like* attending church!" That was certainly a marked and welcome contrast to my childhood religious experience.

As we once again shook Norm's hand on our way out, he said, "Well, this wasn't really a typical service either. We don't usually have a children's service and a baptism."

I was ready this time. "Oh, I supposed that happens maybe, say, once a month?"

"That sounds about right," Norm said. "Once a month. You should probably come back next week to see a regular service."

As we drove out of the parking lot, and passed the two other Lutheran churches we hadn't even set foot inside of yet, I said, "Well, Daddy, you want to try Trinity or Zion next week?"

"Why would we do that?" Dad responded.

"We still haven't seen a typical service here at Immanuel," I replied. "At the rate we're going, we'll never get to the rest of the Lutheran churches in town."

"I like this one just fine," Dad said. "Don't you?"

"It doesn't matter what I think, does it?" I asked.

"It probably should, since you're going with me every Sunday morning. Unless you plan to just dump me off every week." There was a long pause. "It'd be nice if you liked the church we're going to."

And just like that, I stepped into the snare that I hadn't even realized he had set. Every Sunday morning. Church. How in the world had that happened? And why in the world did I feel so good about it??

White Trash TV

Between driving there and back and the service itself, attending church took up about three hours a week. That left 109 other waking hours that Daddy had to fill. He didn't know anyone, and he wouldn't drive anywhere alone. He would take short walks if I insisted, but it was winter, and mostly he didn't have anything to do or anyone to do it with. As a result, he settled into the old beat up recliner that he had brought with him and watched TV in the living room. All day. Every day. And he didn't hear all that well, so the TV was LOUD! LOUD!! LOUD!!! He began with *The Price Is Right* at 10 a.m. Then it was *The Young and the Restless*. Next *Jerry Springer* would make an appearance. After that he would channel surf or doze with the TV still blaring until 2 p.m. At 2 it was time for *Let's Make a Deal*. At 3 it was *Dr. Phil*. At 4 he would reluctantly watch *The Ellen DeGeneres Show* with me. Then it was the local news, followed by the national news, followed by the local news again. Next came *Jeopardy* and *Wheel of Fortune*. By the time Homer came home from work, Daddy was chuckling at mindless sitcoms filled with sexual innuendos that I used to enjoy but now found embarrassing to be viewing with my dad. Some nights he watched reruns of *Walker, Texas Ranger* or other oldies that weren't really very good the first time around. And I believe I mentioned that it was always LOUD! LOUD!! LOUD!!!

Several months before Dad arrived, Homer had said wistfully one night, "The nice thing about your Dad moving in is I'm going to finally have someone to watch Westerns with." I think he had a picture in his head of two ol' boys in their respective recliners reveling in John Wayne and Clint Eastwood movies, bonding until the wee hours of the morning. He didn't expect his home to be invaded by screaming game show contestants, screaming dysfunctional couples, and screaming laugh tracks. It only took a couple weeks of this, followed by weekends of endless televised football, rodeos, ice dancing, and *Lawrence Welk*, for Homer to go off the deep end.

"Let's take a walk," he said to me one Sunday afternoon. This would all-too-soon become code for, "Your dad's driving me crazy. We need to talk. Alone." We left the house and could still hear the TV blaring as we made our way down the long driveway. Once safely out of earshot, Homer said, "I can't stand it. All he does is watch white trash TV all day, every day. He doesn't do *anything* else. And the junk he watches. My God!!! It's all mindless garbage that a six-year-old wouldn't even find interesting. And why does it have to be so damn loud!?! I can't hear myself think. We haven't had a moment's silence since he moved in. Except when he's sleeping. And even then, the TV's on half the time!! What the hell are we going to do?"

"What do you think he should be doing?" I asked.

"I don't give a damn," Homer muttered. "*Anything* would be better than this."

"Like what?" I asked. "It's the dead of winter. He can't walk on the icy roads. He doesn't hunt or trap anymore. He can't garden. He doesn't know anyone. He doesn't want to hang out at the Senior Citizen Center with a bunch of strangers. He doesn't gamble, so the casino is out. He doesn't like to go to movies. Except for us, all the rest of his family is a hundred miles away. Exactly what would you suggest that he do?"

"I don't know," Homer growled, "but you better think of something. That TV noise is driving me nuts. And it's not helping his mind any either."

There was truth to what he said. Daddy needed to be engaged in something more stimulating than watching television day in and day out. But what? I thought back to his reading my book about Mom when he first moved in. Hmmm. That was an idea. When we were kids, he was never one for books, but Mom subscribed to *Outdoor Life; Fur, Fish, and Game;* and *Reader's Digest*, and he regularly read all of them. After my mom died, he let all those subscriptions lapse. Once he married Ruth, he had stayed busy, so he pretty much stopped reading altogether. Maybe I could change that.

I stopped in at school the next day and picked up a couple of books I thought my dad might enjoy. He had always loved the outdoors, so I borrowed *Call of the Wild* and *White Fang* for starters. I got permission to bring them back whenever he finished them—no rush, since the school had multiple copies. I returned home with the two relatively short paperbacks in hand, hoping they would not be too daunting for a man who had only an eighth-grade education. I handed them to Dad and said, "Give these a try. I think you might like them." Imagine my surprise when the next afternoon Daddy turned off the TV and read for over an hour in blessed silence. By the end of the week he had powered through both of them and said I should return them. "Want me to get you some more?" I asked. "That'd be OK," he said. "They were good." So, Friday I exchanged them for three more paperbacks, returned home, and handed them over.

Thus began my father's new-found love of books. I continued to borrow books from school until I ran out of subject matter that he liked. Then I moved on to the public library, where the selection was much greater. Every week I'd check out first two, then three, then four or more books for Dad to read. He'd devour them one by one, and then we'd repeat the ritual. After about six months, I noticed it was taking him longer and longer to finish a book. I wondered about this. I saw him squinting, and I suspected that his glaucoma was making his eyesight worse. I knew that he was unlikely to bring it up on his own, so I checked out a large print book for him to try. "Oh, that's more like it," he said. "Finally, the words ain't so small. Get me this kind from now on." He resumed his voracious reading, now all large print library books. In due course, he made his way through nearly every one of the Rhinelander District Library's large print titles that appealed to him. Fortunately, the inter-library loan system gave us access to large print books from all the libraries in the area, so I was able to keep him well supplied. He continued to read until shortly before his death.

He still watched *The Price Is Right*, *Dr. Phil*, and the news, and the volume was still loud, loud, loud, but there were long stretches of silence in between. His mind was active, we had books to talk about, and Homer and I had back a bit of our old, peaceful life.

It's in the Cards

Wisconsin winter days are very short and very dark, and the long nights sometimes seem interminable. When we were kids growing up, after chores my family often gathered around the kitchen table on winter evenings, eating popcorn, drinking Kool-Aid, and playing cards. My dad was an excellent card player, and he especially enjoyed 500 Rummy and Sheepshead. I learned both games at an early age just by watching, and I very much enjoyed this simple recreation. It was one of the few times when we all played, rather than worked, together.

Except for chess and Scrabble, Homer has never been much of a game player, but he knows his share of card games. One winter night when there was nothing any of us wanted to watch on TV, I suggested a game of cards. Both my dad and Homer reluctantly pried themselves out of their recliners and moved into the kitchen. I dug out a dusty deck of cards, counted to make sure they were all there, and pulled out the cards needed for Sheepshead. That night I dealt the first of what would eventually become many hands in an on-going Sheepshead tournament.

None of us had played for a while, but Daddy had over eight decades of experience, so he had the edge at first. He was a card counter, knew how many trump and fail had been played, how many points everybody had, and was excellent at deducing what cards we had left in our hands. I did all right for a while, since I had played this game most of my life. Homer hadn't learned until he met me, so he was at a decided disadvantage. But not for long. He has a mathematical, analytical mind, and after a few weeks had gone by, he was playing much better than I was. It became a battle of will, strategy, and luck between him and my dad. I was basically in the room to ensure someone other than the two of them would come in dead last and to provide comic relief.

Occasionally things would get a little *too* competitive, and I would have to remind one or both of them that this was supposed to be fun. Most of the time it was, but it subtly changed over time. Our card games were an interesting weekly barometer measuring how much Homer and Daddy were getting on each other's nerves. The tension was hidden under seemingly good-natured barbs and insults, but it was there, rarely at first, but gradually as the newness of our living arrangement changed, the banter became more acrimonious than it once had been. When that would happen, I used the next day to privately suss out what was really bothering them. Then I would do my best to troubleshoot. It was a strange but effective mediation strategy, and it worked for many months. Eventually, however, it would not be enough.

Despite their occasional flares of temper, I very much enjoyed these card games, and it was always I who suggested that we play. For a year and a half, we whiled away the evenings with this post-dinner activity. I had no idea how much I would come to miss losing at Sheepshead to my two favorite men.

Dancing Again

My father was born to dance. He liked to waltz and polka, but above all, he loved to square dance. My mother did not share his enthusiasm for dance, but she eventually learned, just to please Dad. When we were kids, my father eagerly looked forward to dancing every Saturday night. Sundays he spent singing the refrains, reciting the calls, and doing a play-by-play of favorite dances that went extremely well and new ones that people were struggling to learn. It was a crushing disappointment to him when my mother's failing health ended her dancing. She encouraged him to go without her, but he did not, even though he missed it and remembered it fondly.

After my mother died, I could see that my father needed a social outlet. John Dittner, a square dance caller whom my dad liked very much, had attended Mom's funeral and invited Dad to come to the weekly Marshfield Senior Citizen Center square dances. I urged Daddy to follow through, and within a few months, he was dancing regularly again. He got to know several widows who also attended, dated a couple, and eventually met, fell in love with, and married Ruth. They were "Golden Squares" fixtures, and it seemed nothing would slow them down. That remained true until Ruth suffered her stroke and was wheelchair bound. She recognized how much Daddy enjoyed dancing, so she would accompany him to the dances, watch as he moved around the square, and socialize with those sitting out. When it became too difficult for her to attend, she urged Daddy to continue to go alone. Other than church and visits from family, it was the only time he socialized. I went with him a time or two when I was home visiting, and I loved seeing the pride and delight on his face as he followed the calls without hesitation or mistakes. After Ruth died, I accompanied him several more times, and the other dancers often encouraged me to join in, but I was prepared with my excuses. I felt this was my father's time to focus solely on his beloved friends. I would go off to run errands and shop and arrive back just in time for the final dance, of which they insisted I be a part. Dad's friends were disappointed but supportive when he decided to move to Rhinelander. They threw him a farewell party and made me promise to bring him to Marshfield as often as possible to dance. I agreed. Every couple of months, we'd make the trip back home so he could join them. It was two hundred miles of driving 'round trip, but it was worth it. We'd incorporate a haircut by his hometown barber and a visit to Ruth's family as well, so it made for a full day. It gave him something to anticipate and remember, and he, usually a man of few words, had much to talk about as we drove home in the fading light.

 It seemed to me that we needed to find square dancing opportunities closer to home for him as well. I discovered there was a little club in Rhinelander called The Hodag Twirlers that was looking for members. It took a while to talk Dad into going, but eventually he did. Although he was one of the oldest people there, he was also one of the most accomplished dancers, and they welcomed him warmly. I would drive him into town, park, walk in with him carrying the treats I'd baked to share when it was his turn, and then leave him for a couple of hours of dancing.

About half an hour before they were finished, I'd return to chat with the other dancers a bit and then escort Dad back out to the car. Admittedly, these evenings weren't as special to him as his Marshfield excursions, but they gave him an additional opportunity to dance as well as foster new relationships in Rhinelander. He'd record on the calendar the dates of upcoming dances and remind me as they approached, so I knew he looked forward to these outings.

Church, reading, card playing, and dancing were gradually giving shape to Dad's new life in Rhinelander. Needless to say, they were also reshaping mine.

On the Road

I knew that Daddy had occasional medical appointments, but I had no idea how many there were and how difficult it would be to work them around my consulting schedule. I had contracts with four different charter schools which required me to typically spend a day or two in each of them every month. Those mornings, I would get up early, drive a hundred plus miles to the school, spend the day with students and staff, the night in a hotel, another day at another school in the area, and then drive home. Since the schedule was unpredictable, I often didn't know much more than a day or two in advance when and where I was going. Daddy's medical maintenance, on the other hand, was routine, relentless, and inflexible.

He saw six different physicians in three different towns. His internist was responsible for overseeing his overall care, and we drove thirty miles to Woodruff twice a year to see him unless Daddy had issues in between. Because he had advanced glaucoma, he also saw an ophthalmologist in Woodruff every three months. That doctor always ran behind. In addition to our travel time, we would often wait for over an hour to get in to see him. The renal specialist also worked out of Woodruff, but he came to Rhinelander once a month to see patients, so we were usually able to schedule appointments closer to home, but it was still a twenty-five-minute drive. These appointments required regular lab work, too, and frequent follow-ups, so Dr. Flannigan, his nurse, Daddy, and I got to be very, very well acquainted over time. We saw Dr. Flannigan every other month, and sometimes in between.

In addition to visiting his kidney specialist, Daddy also saw a dermatologist in Rhinelander every six months. Dad had spent his lifetime farming outdoors, and he had any number of pre-cancerous spots on his face that had to be monitored and removed as needed. He also had regular podiatry appointments to have his toenails trimmed, a task I was very glad to delegate to someone else.

Most time-consuming of all were the trips every six months to the VA hospital in Iron Mountain, Michigan. It took two hours to drive there, two or more hours waiting for a ten-minute appointment, and another two hours more to return home. These were long days to which neither of us looked forward, but my father had been told it was necessary for the VA to provide his eye drops. Eventually I asked why the Minocqua ophthalmologist couldn't share his findings with the VA, and lo and behold, we discovered that he indeed could and should have been doing so. Unfortunately, it took three unnecessary four hundred-mile trips until I finally had the sense to raise the question.

Most of these appointments resulted in subsequent pharmacy runs. Dad regularly needed over-the-counter drugs along with the prescription medications, so I also spent a lot of time at Walgreens. Once I brought home what he needed, however, he took over. Most of his prescriptions were routinely mailed to him. He'd unpackage them and then line his medicines up on his dresser in the order in which they needed to be taken. Every Sunday the dining room would resound with the clatter of his pill splitter as he sat at the table halving meds as needed for the week. He knew exactly what, how many, and when to administer his drugs or use his eye drops, and he was religious about it. If he knew we would be away from home for any length of time, he tucked whatever he needed into his pocket. I rarely needed to remind him to take anything. I'd keep an eye on the bottles on his dresser to make sure he wasn't running low and reorder if necessary, but otherwise, he was in charge. It was wonderful to know that I could count on him in this regard. It was more than enough for me just to juggle the regular appointments. I can't imagine what life would have been like if I had had to manage his meds and he had opted for dialysis as well.

SPRING

Daddy at Arlington, April 2012

A Place in the Sun

Dad spent most of the winter huddled next to the fireplace. One of his symptoms of renal failure was feeling cold all the time. No matter how many layers he wore, he was still freezing. Typically, visitors would walk into our seventy-degree house and see Dad in his recliner under an electric blanket, wearing a winter coat over a sweatshirt over a flannel shirt over a t-shirt, a wool hat, flannel lined jeans, and heavy work shoes. He positioned himself as close to the wood-burning stove as possible without setting his recliner on fire. The little dogs seemed to know that he couldn't get warm, so one would lie on his lap while the other perched on the back of his chair, draped around his neck like a furry white stole. He divided his time between watching the deer that came in to feed in the front yard and dozing in his chair, dreaming of warmer days.

Apparently, those were powerful dreams, because spring came early in 2012. Temperatures in March were unseasonably high, and the snow soon disappeared. It is not unusual for us to still have snow on the ground in late April, so this was a rare and wonderful occurrence indeed. "Just wait," Homer and I both warned him. "Old

Man Winter is only on hiatus and will come roaring back in a week or two." But we were wrong. The days stayed warm and sunny, the robins returned, and Dad moved from his recliner to a wooden glider on the front porch. He'd sit there in his many layers, reading and soaking up the sun. The dogs lay at his feet keeping him company, and for the first time since he'd moved in with us, I thought he was, if not happy, at least content. Spring was here, summer was coming, and he was finally looking forward, as well as back. "This is working," I thought. "This is working."

Never Forgotten

Shortly after my dad moved in, I learned about the Never Forgotten Honor Flight. This non-profit central Wisconsin program provides free Washington D.C. day trips to veterans four times a year. In total, almost four hundred area veterans from World War II, the Korean, and Vietnam conflicts are recognized annually by visits to the Washington D.C. memorials established in their honor. My friend Karen's father had been part of the September 2011 trip, and she couldn't say enough about what a great time he had had. I thought since Dad was still physically able to travel, he ought to apply. If he was accepted and wasn't well enough to go when the time came, someone else could take his place. I explained it all to Dad and asked him if he was interested. "That sounds all right," Daddy said with his usual deadpan expression. "But *you* gotta fill out all the paperwork."

I did so. Every veteran is accompanied by a "guardian" on the flight, who makes sure the vet is looked after throughout the trip. Sometimes these are family members, but often they are strangers who volunteer and pay their own way to accompany a veteran to recognize his or her service. I decided to apply to be my dad's guardian. The cost was reasonable, and I knew he'd feel better about the trip if I went with him. There was no guarantee of either of us being selected, but World War II veterans are given preference, as is anyone with a terminal illness, and Dad fit into both categories. I finished the paperwork and sent it on in. A month or so later we received a call from one of the Flight volunteers. He chatted Daddy up, and asked several questions about his physical condition, one of them being could he walk the length of a football field, or did he need a wheelchair for that? Daddy proudly said he could do that, and that he never used a wheelchair, or even a walker. When asked, he also assured the volunteer that he could climb up and down bus steps without the use of a lift. The volunteer said Dad would hear from the organization in the next few weeks about their decision. The following month we learned that both Daddy and I had been selected for the April 2012 flight. I was very excited, but Dad simply said, "Well, that's nice." Anticipating the trip made the last months of winter easier to bear, at least for me.

April 21 finally arrived. Although the actual flight would be Monday, on Sunday afternoon I needed to attend required guardian training. The evening would feature a banquet for the veterans and their families. Dad and I checked in at Howard Johnson's in Wausau around 1:30. Smiling volunteers handed us our t-shirts, jackets, and fanny packs stuffed with disposable cameras. After Dad settled into our hotel room, which was also provided free of charge for anyone traveling more than thirty miles, I headed off to the training.

Many guardians, including me, were responsible for two veterans, one often being a family member, and the second being someone we would meet for the first time. Volunteers stressed that veterans flying alone should be made to feel as much like family as the blood relative with whom you were traveling. At no time should the veteran feel ignored or less important; both should receive equal time, attention, and kindness. In addition to my dad, I was assigned to Robert Hein, a World War II vet from Wisconsin Rapids. That meant I was responsible for two of the forty World War II vets on the flight. After my training session ended, I woke Dad up from his nap, and we went to sit in the lobby, Dad on the watch for Dale and Rosann who were joining us for the pre-flight dinner, me on the lookout for Robert Hein.

I felt a little like I was about to go on a blind date. "What will he look like? What are we going to talk about? Are we going to get along OK?" All these questions and more raced through my mind as I waited. I didn't wait long. Robert walked towards me with his wife, and he looked in pretty good shape. I spied his name tag as he spied mine, and I greeted him with a handshake that quickly morphed into a hug. He was all smiles, and I knew at once that this was going to be a good match. I was already sure that my ninety-year-old dad wouldn't be able to handle a full day of walking around Washington and would need a wheelchair, but it appeared that Robert was ambulatory, and that set my fears at ease about how I would care for two guys at once. Robert's wife would remain in Wausau when we traveled to D.C.

Once Dale and Rosann arrived, the six of us moved into the dining room for a night of speeches, entertainment, and dinner. It was a lovely evening, and I got to know Robert and his wife a little better. At the end of the night, each vet received a care package full of gifts that people had sent from all over the United States. Bursting with little items ranging from a tooth-brush, mouthwash, comb, tissues, gum, and candy to a handmade scarf and thank you letters, the contents tickled Daddy and Robert. It was well past Dad's usual bedtime when the evening was finally over, and we said good night to everyone. Although the wake-up call was scheduled for 4 a.m., Dad wanted to be up by 3:15. I knew I should head to bed too, but I wasn't ready. I had learned during dinner that Robert would require oxygen and a wheelchair all day. That rekindled my worries about how I would manage two of them in chairs. Someone had assured me there would be others to help, but I still couldn't get to sleep thinking about it. I grabbed my book and found a quiet spot in the lobby to read. It was after 1:00 when I finally got to bed. I knew it would be a very short night before a very long day.

Two hours later we were up and at 'em just after 3. Dad wanted to ride with me to the airport in my car rather than join Robert and his wife on the bus. It turns out Dad should have taken the bus, too, because we had to walk about a quarter of a mile across the parking lot in the early morning darkness and rain. He was already exhausted by the time we got to the door, so I put him in the first wheelchair of the day. It was true that Dad could walk the length of a football field–but only once. I guessed there were going to be a lot of "football fields" that day. We passed through security, and then we breakfasted on donuts, fruit, coffee and juice. After kissing their spouses goodbye, the veterans boarded the plane. As we taxied down the runway, water cannons on either side of the plane launched plumes of water over us to send us on our way. I don't think anyone slept on the almost two-hour flight to D.C. Everybody was so full of anticipation about the day that it didn't matter that they'd gotten up so early. There was another water cannon salute as we landed.

"Washington D.C.!!" one of the veterans said in disbelief. Once the plane stopped, we gathered wheelchairs and seated the guys who needed them. Then the doors opened, and away we went. We were greeted by a crowd of people lined up on either side, applauding, waving signs, thanking the vets for their service, and reaching out to shake hands while someone played military songs. Everywhere we went in the airport, people stopped and talked to the vets. We were hard to miss—the vets a sea of bright yellow jackets, polo shirts and Honor

Flight caps, the guardians hovering nearby dressed identically in green. The first few Honor Flight colors were red and blue, but after the Packers played in the Super Bowl, they decided green and gold made a bolder Wisconsin statement. Dad had pulled his yellow wind breaker on over the top of his bulky winter parka. He looked a little like a stuffed sausage, but it made him easy to spot.

After boarding three buses, our first destination was the WW II Memorial. Then it was time for a bus tour of the Capitol, Navy Memorial, and White House–all while enjoying a huge box lunch. We arrived next at the Korean, Vietnam, and Lincoln Memorials. By this time, despite his seventy-two layers of clothes and parka, my dad was shivering in the April wind, but off we went to see the Vietnam Memorial. As I wheeled Dad along the wall with its 58,000 plus names of casualties, I could see his reflection moving across the names, a ninety-year-old man huddled in his wheelchair, grateful to still be alive when so many who came after him had already died. There but for the grace of God...

Then we were back on the bus for a snack, another of the requisite roll calls, and a drive past the Pentagon and the scarred wall where the terrorist plane had crashed. That was a scary, sobering reminder of a dark, dark day. From there it was on to the Air Force Memorial, three soaring spires on a hillside overlooking Arlington National Cemetery.

By now it was 4:30 eastern time. We had been in Washington about six hours, and Arlington was next. We arrived in time for the Changing of the Guard at the Tomb of the Unknown Soldier. I expected Dad to be impressed by the pomp and circumstance and solemnity of the ceremony. Later he said, "That was my least favorite part. Three guys marching up and down. Seems kind of stupid to me." But he so loved the rows and rows of white tombstones, and especially a few cherry trees that were still in bloom, that I was inspired to write a poem that appears at the end of this chapter.

Our last stop on the tour was the Iwo Jima Memorial, which we'd passed by many times that day. By this late in the afternoon, increasing numbers of veterans were allowing themselves to be pushed in wheelchairs, and at each stop, one or two more opted to stay on the bus. "Come on, Dad," I said. "Nope," Dad said, "I'm staying put. It's too damn cold out there."

"Aw, come on," I started to plead.

Dad gave me "the look" and said, "I said no." There was a long, uncomfortable silence. He turned to the others who were waiting to see how this standoff would pan out, and said, "She's my daughter. I can talk to her like that."

"Yep," I said, "Can and does. Suit yourself," I conceded as I followed Robert down the bus aisle. There was one last group photo in front of the statue of the six flag raisers. Maybe if Dad had known that, he would have ventured forth, but maybe not. Cold is cold, and he was so tired of it. Not only that, he was just plain tired. It had already been a very long day. On the way back to the airport, yet another round of boxed lunches was handed out. "One thing about this trip," Dad said. "If you go hungry, you don't have anybody to blame but yourself."

At Reagan Airport we went through another perfunctory security check and boarded the plane. It was 9 o'clock at night now, and we'd been riding an emotional roller coaster for seventeen hours. You would have thought when the plane lifted off and the lights went out, it would have been a snooze fest. Instead, there was a quiet, steady murmur as vets and guardians processed the day's events. I didn't see a single person sleeping. The flight crew passed out cookies in baggies, each containing a note of thanks, and then one of leaders announced over the PA, "Well, I'll bet there's at least one good memory every one of you has about being in the service. That's mail call. This trip wouldn't be complete without some letters from home. When I call your name, raise your hand. Guardians, I could use your help." Guardians throughout the plane stood up and formed a mail call assembly line down the center aisle. 99 manila envelopes bulging with mail along with 99 boxes of Girl Scout cookies moved from the front to the back of the plane as name after name was called. I watched my dad's expectant face, waiting, waiting, like a kid at Christmas, so hoping he'd been a good enough boy, so wanting not to be overlooked. "LaVerne Machtan," the voice called, and Daddy raised his arthritic hand and grinned. He didn't open the envelope. He didn't open the cookies. He just held them tightly in his hands and smiled his little smile. He told me later he didn't want to lose any of the letters, so he'd wait until the next day at the hotel, when he was wide awake and sitting still to read them. All those letters people took the time to write meant so much to him.

Mail call made the rest of the trip seem very short, even though it was after 10 o'clock when we finally deplaned in Mosinee. As in D.C., a welcoming committee was waiting for us, but this time it was huge, hundreds of people, many of them whom the veterans knew, friends and family waving signs and photos and flags, a full brass band playing military songs, cameras flashing, hands and arms outstretched. I was grinning from ear to ear, and Dad was quietly saying, "Thank you, thank you," all the while clutching his letters and box of cookies. Ruth's kids, Jean and Richard, along with their spouses, Ronnie and Dee, were there to greet Dad, and he was surprised and delighted to see them. Every other vet had a welcoming committee too. It would be impossible to measure the level of excitement and gratitude that filled that airport. It didn't matter if it was the first guy off the plane, or the last one, the applause was steady and loud.

At the end of the gauntlet stood a group of bearded, tattooed, leathered bikers, looking tough on the outside but squishy on the inside. They waited until the buses were filled, then headed out into the pouring rain and wind and darkness to provide a motorcycle escort back to the hotel. I wanted Dad to be part of that, so I had him take the bus while I drove back to Howard Johnson's. I watched the bikers come roaring up with the buses and then joined them to help wrangle wheel chairs while the veterans got off the bus. Someone asked one of the bikers how the ride was, and as the rain streamed off his bandanna and down his face, he said, "Exhilarating." And he meant it.

By the time we were headed to our rooms, Dad, along with everyone else, was exhausted. As we shuffled along with Robert and his wife and the others, I said, "Well, it's 11:30. Remember, reveille is at 1:30." Several of them looked at me as if I'd lost my mind, but Dad didn't miss a beat. "Buuuuuuuuullshit!" he declared.

"OK, OK," I said. "I guess you can sleep in."

"Damn right," he said.

I, however, was too wired once again to sleep. I saw him safely to bed, then took my phone and my book and headed for the bar for a glass of wine. Two, actually. I spent the next couple of hours thinking about all that had happened, the words that I wanted to write spinning in my head, and a poem or two taking shape that I was too tired to put to paper. By two in the morning I finally fell asleep. The next day Dad slept in while I drove to a meeting in Stevens Point. I got back to the hotel around 4:30, and Dad was napping. He had the heat turned up high, had read all his letters, and he was one satisfied fella. We were both ready to drive back home. We had had an excellent adventure that neither one of us we would ever forget.

Never Forgotten

My father's favorite Washington war memorial:
Cherry blossoms.
Not granite or bronze renderings,
marble obelisks,
larger than life presidents
or reflecting pools.
Not a wall of 58,000 names that scars the earth
or the platoon of nineteen still on Korean patrol.
Not the valiant six at Iwo Jima,
not even the orderly
endless white tombstone soldiers
row on row
marching for eternity.

My father's flag is woven
from cherry blossoms,
the last ones,
the ones that linger,
late blooming,
fragile sentinels of spring,
foreign pink gnarled fists that
sadly
will too soon disappear.

The ground is littered
with their remnants,
but he looks up.
Cherry blossoms.
He breathes.
Take a picture of this.
This is what I came to see.
They were supposed
to be gone by now, he says,

but some things last.
He grins into the camera,
shoulders hunched against the wind,
wheelchair proud—
a silent one-man salute
to cherry blossoms

SUMMER

Daddy being helped out after B-17 Bomber flight, 2012

Glad All Over

Daddy had been an avid gardener his entire adult life, and while he grew the requisite lettuce, tomatoes, and cucumbers, the driving force behind his garden was his beloved gladiola. Even when he was busy running his dairy farm, he managed to grow a breath-taking array of the lovely tall spikes of color. He entered them every year at the Central Wisconsin State fair open class flower competition and invariably walked away with blue ribbons. Fan-shaped vases of glads graced our kitchen table throughout August and September, and I assumed these flowers were part of everyone's end of summer rituals. It wasn't until I tried to grow them myself that I discovered just how difficult and time-consuming a passion these truly are. After several failed attempts to grow them in our Northwoods sandy soil during much-too short seasons, I resigned myself to purchasing rather than planting them. I have always loved these flowers, though, and even carried them in my December wedding bouquet when roses and stephanotis would have been much less expensive.

I assumed Daddy would want to continue gardening to some extent after moving in with us, but he had hung up his trowel with the same conviction as he put away his driver's license. When I told him we had to at least plant some glads, he said, "You go right ahead. I'm done with that." But he couldn't resist overseeing the process and chortling over my ineptitude, and so it was, after the obligatory soaking of his last year's bulbs in a mixture of Lysol water to kill "those damned thrips" (a mysterious scourge I have never understood), we found ourselves in the garden on Memorial Day. Frosts come late and linger where we live, but Memorial Day is generally safe for planting. This one was unusually hot and humid, with rain threatening–an ideal time to get bulbs in the soil.

I had dragged hoes and rakes and bulbs out to the patch Homer had cleared for a garden. Despite the truck load of compost we had hauled in, the ground was poor and unpromising. I started digging the first trench for my glads, and Dad just shook his head. "What's the problem?" I asked, looking at the jagged shallow furrow I had made.

"That's crookeder than a dog's hind leg!" Dad said. "Where's your stake and string to mark this so you get a straight line?"

"Oh, is that how you do it?" I said.

Another shake of his head. "I can see this ain't gonna be easy," he said. "You sure ain't no glad person."

I filled in my first attempt at a row, and under his tutelage managed to dig four straight long trenches for bulbs. He supervised while I carefully placed each bulb right side up and equidistant apart. By this time the thunder was rolling, and lightening had started to flash. "You'd better head to the house," I told him. "The storm's coming fast."

"Ha!" he scoffed. "And leave you here alone? I'd better stick around and keep an eye on you."

I hurried to get the rest of the bulbs in the dirt and then, under his scrutiny, covered them.

The wind was picking up, the clouds were scudding across the sky, and Homer said as he trotted past, "Come on, you two. Time to head inside."

I looked at Dad, and he said, "Finish." I had one row left to cover when the heavens opened, and the deluge started. I hurried to get the final row done as the cold rain pelted us both. When I was done, Dad shuffled along beside me and we hunkered down under the overhanging branches of a tree, waiting for it to lighten up enough to make the trip back to the house. It didn't, at least not for a long time. When we finally got to the garage, water was running off our hair and down our backs, our clothes were soaked, and our shoes were waterlogged. At that point it was too late to run, so we just trudged along, rake and hoe and empty glad bucket in hand. Homer opened the door and said, "Get in here! What the hell were you two thinking?"

"Glads need a good soaking when you first plant 'em," Dad said. "They got one."

Summer passed, and the glads grew, and those four rows seemed to get longer with every weeding. I felt compelled to at least try after what we went through to plant them, but my heart wasn't in it. By the end of June, Daddy started asking when I planned to hill them. Hilling is required to make sure glads stand erect when they start blooming, since the heavy flowers otherwise cause the stalks to bend under their weight. I assured Dad I would get to it in the next week or so. But, to be honest, it wasn't as high on my priority list as it was his. One blistering afternoon in mid-July I came home after running errands. When I went into the house, Dad was nowhere to be found. I called and called, but there was no answer. The dogs didn't seem to know where he was, and panic quickly set in. Had he fallen somewhere? I checked all the rooms, the back and front yards—no Dad. I headed to the road to see if he was out for a walk, and as I passed the path to the garden, it occurred to me. No, I told myself–he wouldn't.

But oh yes, he would. There he was, on his hands and knees, finishing hilling the last row of glads. Each row had been carefully weeded, and all the spires were standing tall and straight, evenly hilled from the left and right sides after hours of back-breaking labor. He was sweating like crazy, and I said, "What the helllll are you doing?"

"What the hell does it look like?" he shot back. "Hilling your glads."

"I said I was going to get to it!" I protested. "Why today of all days? It must be a hundred degrees out here!!"

"Well, you didn't get to it," he said. "And it needed to be done. Now help me up. I've been on my knees so long, I can't stand."

That was one of the days I could have easily won the Worst Daughter Ever trophy.

The glads were late blooming, and the flowers never grew to the size his would have. Although they were beautiful by early September, they paled in comparison with his past efforts. I dutifully dug the bulbs, dried them, and kept them cool in the basement throughout the following winter for planting the next spring, but I wondered why I hadn't simply conceded defeat right then. He was absolutely correct. I ain't no glad person.

Flying High

Ken had mentioned Dad's Honor Flight to a friend of his in Madison who was very involved in the annual B-17 Heavy Bombers Weekend. This event featured a display of World War II bombers during the day at the Dane County Airport and a Hangar Dance fund raiser for the Badger Honor Flight in the evening. Ken's friend Don Winkler knew that Dad had been in the Army Air Corps during World War II and told Ken he could get Daddy on one of the B-17 flights if Dad were interested. We all thought it would be a thrill for Dad to finally fly in one of these old planes that he had spent so much time around during the war.

Dad agreed to the outing, and so on July 26, 2012, he found himself once again being pushed in a wheelchair through an airport crowded with veterans and then out onto the tarmac to admire these beautiful old planes. Ken accompanied him onto the bomber for a flight around Madison. Ken, who is six feet four inches tall, struggled to pretzel himself into the little hatchway, and I was afraid it would take a can opener to get my dad on and off the plane, but somehow, they managed. He and several other octogenarians and family members eventually were all on board. The plane rumbled down the runway, and then lifted off. Other guests waited with us while they took a scenic flight over the Capitol, Madison lakes, and outlying farmland. When the plane once again touched down, and the cargo of veterans were pried free, several television reporters descended upon them for "How did it feel?" interviews. Dad's welcoming grin attracted one pretty, young woman and a cameraman for whom I instantly felt very sorry.

"Hi!" she said as she reached out to shake his hand. "I'm from Channel 3 here in Madison, and I'm wondering if I could interview you."

"Oh no, oh no, oh no," I thought. "This is going to be a disaster. She has no idea he isn't going to say anything. He's just going to smile and give her one-word answers and nods."

He looked at me, and I repeated what she had said. "Oh sure," he grinned.

"Great!!" she chirped. "Just give us a minute to set up here."

"Um, he isn't much of a talker," I said, which was certainly an understatement.

"Oh, no problem," she said. "I'm used to that."

Ken had a stricken look on his face, but I figured since he got to do the flight, he could have the privilege of the interview, too.

She asked for their names. That was the only easy response of the whole ordeal.

"So," she began, "you are a veteran, correct?"

"Yup," he said.

"Can you describe your service?"

"Army."

"Um...did you ever fly in one of these planes?"

"Nope."

"Oh.... well, how was the flight today?"

"Real good."

"Hmmmm, how did you end up serving during World War II?"

"What?"

"How'd you end up in the Army, Dad?" I coached.

"Oh," he said. "I got me a letter in the mail one day. It said, 'Uncle Sam wants you.' So, I went."

By this time the reporter knew she had picked an affable mark, but one who simply had nothing to say. She ended the interview as quickly and politely as possible, and as she was packing up, I said, "I'm sorry. He wasn't trying to give you a hard time. He just never has much to say."

"Well," she laughed. "You tried to warn me. We've got enough footage to get a story. It will be on tomorrow."

The next day on the news, there sat Daddy in his wheelchair, looking at the camera saying, "'Uncle Sam wants you.' So, I went." Ken and I still have a copy of that interview. And it still makes us laugh. We thought we had arranged for an experience of a lifetime for Dad, but he would have been just as happy sitting in his recliner. Still, it probably was better than hilling glads.

On the Road Again

Shortly after Daddy moved in, I asked him if there was anywhere he wanted to go or anything he wanted to do before he died. "Not really," he said.

"Are you sure?" I pushed. "Because you're still healthy enough to do just about anything you want. Isn't there someone you'd like to visit?"

"Well," he said. "I guess I'd kind of like to visit Neal in Kansas one last time. I always liked him."

Neal was my mother's last living brother, and he was my dad's favorite. When Dad had been stationed in Kansas during World War II, Neal and Daddy would often go hunting together. It was not uncommon for Neal to drive the old Model A while Daddy rode on the fender, rifle at the ready to pick off unsuspecting rabbits and pheasants that fled at the noise of the jalopy. They had plenty of stories of the old days, and I think Daddy enjoyed visits with Mom's brother at least as much as she did.

And so, Daddy's next excellent adventure was set into motion. Homer didn't want to miss work for a week-long trip to Kansas, especially in August, and I thought it wouldn't be wise to travel with Dad alone, so I asked Ken if he'd like to go, and he readily agreed. We checked on flights and found it was relatively inexpensive and fast to fly from Madison to Denver, where we would rent a car to drive to Uncle Neal's farm in western Kansas. Dad and I drove to Ken's the night before the flight and left Madison mid-morning the next day.

Flying out of the Madison airport was easy, with friendly staff and security workers. The flight was painless, and we picked up our rental car and left Denver without a hitch. Daddy was tired by the time we checked into our hotel, but he didn't complain. As soon as we were settled, we headed to my uncle's farm in the country, and then the bullshitting began in earnest. For a man who never had much to say, Daddy held his own, and Ken and I sat back and let their seventy-some years of shared memories and laughter fill the old house. Aunt Retha rustled up sandwiches and iced tea, but the stories went on uninterrupted. It was dark by the time we headed back to our hotel, with my aunt and uncle both disappointed that we wouldn't be staying with them that night. We promised we'd be back after breakfast, and that was enough to get us out the door.

The next several days went by in much the same manner. Between visits, Dad, Ken, and I played cards back at the hotel, something we all really enjoyed. On our last day we all met for lunch at a truck stop across the road. When his regular waitress greeted Uncle Neal, he proudly introduced her to my dad saying, "This is my brother, LaVerne, from Wisconsin."

Aunt Retha immediately corrected him. "He's not your brother," she said. "He's your *brother-in-law*."

"He's my brother as far as I'm concerned," Neal countered. "Always has been."

After lunch we took the obligatory family photos on four different cameras and then said our goodbyes. Daddy and Neal both knew they would probably never see each other alive again, and Neal's eyes misted over as he said, "It was sure good to see you, LaVerne. We had some good old times, didn't we?" Then he turned to Ken and me and said, "You take care of him, y'hear?"

We piled into our rental car, and as I fought to hide my tears. Daddy simply said, "I'm glad we did that. He's quite the Neal."

Our drive to Denver was smooth, albeit quiet. The trouble started when we headed through airport security. Ken was ahead of Daddy and me, and he must have looked law-abiding, because he went through unscathed. Daddy did not fare as well. He warned them that he had had a hip replacement and would set off the metal detector, even had his wallet-sized medical card ready to display. Despite that, when the alarm went off, they pulled him and his cane aside, told me to stay where I was, and ordered him to follow them to a separate room. There they questioned him extensively, had him remove his belt and shoes, patted him down, but stopped short of a strip search. When he hobbled back out to where I was nervously waiting, he was grinning, but I was furious. Did they really think this old gray-haired man was a threat to national security???

My sarcastic nature bubbled to the surface. "Thanks *very* much," I said with a smile to the TSA agent. "I really appreciate you keeping everyone on the flight safe from a ninety-year-old man like this." The agent didn't respond with so much as a shrug. "And it was no trouble at all," I continued. "Actually, I think my dad really enjoyed it. This is more action than he's gotten since his wife died." The agent said nothing, just pushed past me. Dad looked at me and grinned. "Don't get so excited," he said. "Now help me get my shoes back on."

He was tired by the time we landed in Madison that evening, and the airport was mostly deserted. I snagged an abandoned wheelchair and pushed him along while Ken took the steps downstairs to the luggage carousel. I guided the wheelchair into the glassed-in elevator and pushed the button for the ground floor. The elevator stalled in mid-descent, alarms started clanging, and suddenly there we were, hanging between two floors with a small, helpless crowd gathering. Ken looked up at us, shook his head, and continued towards the carousel. I was tired, Dad was tired, the alarm kept howling, and my clever attempt at being a heroic daughter had failed dismally. I was ready to cry, but Daddy just said, "What the hell did you do?? I can't take you anywhere." Maintenance showed up shortly after that, fixed the elevator, and we descended the rest of the way to where Ken was waiting, pretending not to know us. He was happy to go ahead—alone—to get the car. As usual, Dad seemed oblivious to the hullabaloo and said no more about it. Until he got back home. Then he was delighted to share the story at every possible opportunity, and he warned everyone that it wasn't a good idea to get on an elevator with me.

Accordions, All Girl Rock Band, and Daddy

I have been a wanna-be rock star all my life. That dream was a far cry from the accordion-playing kid my father had encouraged me to become. I started taking lessons from my sister-in-law when she and my brother lived with us for a while, and after they moved out, my dad insisted that I continue. Let's just say that the accordion was not my instrument of choice. A guitar would have made me much happier, but my dad was not interested in folk music or rock 'n roll. He wanted to listen to polkas and waltzes, and in me, he had those standards available to him on demand. My brothers rolled their eyes at this latest development in the Daddy's Girl saga, while my dad, usually frugal to the point of being tight-fisted, blithely shelled money out for an accordion and lessons, week after week, month after month, year after year. I practiced every day, and eventually I got pretty good at it, considering I have very little natural musical talent. By the time I was seventeen, my music teacher had left the area, and I inherited her accordion students. I charged two dollars an hour and had six to ten students at any one time. It allowed me to earn a little spending money for college when I'd come home every other weekend to teach. My heart still didn't belong to the accordion, but it did belong to Daddy, so I continued with the squeezebox, feeling like a dork and longing for the day when I'd be holding a guitar instead.

After I graduated from college, married, and started teaching English full-time, I didn't get home as much as I used to, but when I did, Dad always made sure the accordion came with me. It gathered a considerable amount of dust in between, as I was playing less and less. By then I had started piano lessons and was much more interested in spending time on that. When my house burned in 1985, so did my accordion and all my music. I was OK with that. But Daddy wasn't. Every time I went home, he'd say, "Hey Sis, I see in the paper there's an accordion for sale. Wanna go look at it?" I came up with one excuse after another to avoid getting roped into another accordion. My future lay in the piano, and maybe eventually the guitar. It did not hold more accordion jokes and insults and polkas. I knew my dad missed hearing me play, but frankly, I didn't really care about that. After all, if he liked the accordion so much, he could learn to play it himself, right?

Years passed, and to my relief, my father badgered me less and less about the accordion. Then one July night in 1994, I had a very, very vivid dream. It was December, and I was trying to figure out what to get my dad for Christmas. I couldn't think of a single thing that would please him, until my subconscious said, "You know, what he'd really like is to hear you play the accordion. Why don't you?" I awoke from that dream determined to do just that.

Thus began the First Great Accordion Quest. I started placing and replying to ads in the newspaper. Most of the accordions were worn, dusty, or broken. So were most of the owners. Every one of them was quirky and lonesome. They were more interested in talking and hearing me play than they were in selling an instrument that had lain dormant in attics or basements for years. Between July and early December, I met countless sellers and still found nothing that I wanted to own. And then I met Stanley Jankowski. Stanley was a retired gentleman who had decided to divorce the piano accordion and marry a concertina instead. He not only was selling a beautiful instrument, but he was willing to part with his sheet music as well. Finding accordion music is even more difficult than finding the instrument, and I have always required music to play. Stanley and I negotiated the price, and by the week before Christmas, I had an accordion that played better than I did. It had been a long time since I had touched what I once regarded as the instrument of the devil, and I had very little time to practice.

On Christmas Day I smuggled the accordion, stuffed in a gigantic bright yellow garbage bag and tied up with a red bow, into Dad and Mom's house. When it was time to open gifts, I told Dad to close his eyes while I hauled his gift out of its hiding place. I told Dad to keep his eyes closed and just use his hands to try to figure out what it was. "Feels like an accordion to me," he dryly concluded. We opened it together, and Dad was beaming.

"LaVerne," one of my sisters-in-law said in confusion, "are you going to learn how to play the accordion?"

"I don't hafta," he said. "She already knows how."

My brother Ken jumped in. "So, let me get this straight, Darlene. You bought yourself an accordion that you say you're giving to Dad for Christmas, and if he's good, once in a while he can listen to you play it???? I guess that means I'll be 'giving' him a Mercedes convertible next year that I'll actually own but let him ride in occasionally. I see how this works." When he put it that way, it seemed like a pretty stupid idea. But Daddy just sat there grinning, and said, "Shut up and play."

To say this was not my best concert is a gross

understatement. I was rusty and unfamiliar with the music, and I interjected plenty of profanity between the many, many mistakes. Dad did not seem to care. When I finished, he said, "Well, next time will be even better. But you might want to do some practicin' between now and then."

I continued playing for him, and I even bought a second accordion during a trip to the Czech Republic. I left that one at his Spencer home, so I didn't have to haul an accordion back and forth every time I visited. I gradually accumulated more music and a decent level of proficiency, but I preferred to spend time banging away on the used upright piano I'd purchased. In 2010 the house we had rebuilt after the first fire tragically burned to the ground. We again lost everything, including two of our dogs, whose attempted rescue caused Homer to sustain third degree burns on forty percent of his body. He nearly died, but after over a month in the Duluth Burn Center and many skins grafts, he eventually fully recovered. That is a story for another book and another day. We bought a home in a different location, furnished it with the help of many friends, and not long after, I began the Second Great Accordion Quest. By the time Daddy moved in with us, I owned not one, not two, but three accordions, along with a keyboard, and an acoustic guitar.

A couple years before Dad moved in, under the guidance of a gifted musician friend, I started guitar lessons which unfortunately quickly morphed into my playing keyboard for a garage band of other women rock star wanna be's, who already had someone on lead guitar. By the time Daddy arrived, the four women who comprised All Girl Rock Band practiced regularly for occasional gigs. We were all fifty or older, so "girl" was a stretch, but the euphemism made us and our small following laugh. So did most of our music, and not always as a result of expertise, but it was a fun hobby. Daddy had never been a fan of contemporary music, but I was his daughter, after all. He sat in on our weekly band practices and dutifully attended our gigs in local bars. I played private accordion concerts for him at home in between, and that was enough to offset the cacophony of Lada Gaga and Creedence Clearwater Revival. And he loved our lead guitarist Sue's voice. While he never complimented me on my performances, he would regularly say of Sue, "Now *that* girl can really sing! And she can do just about everything else too!" Sue both taught full-time and owned a hobby farm, and Daddy delighted chatting with her during our practices or her frequent visits. Whether the topic was castrating calves, repairing tractors, baling hay, or cleaning fish, Sue had stories that tickled Dad. He liked our drummer and bass player too, but he had a special bond with Sue. Dad never missed an All Girl Rock Band practice or a gig, and even though he never really liked most of our music, he was our biggest groupie. Despite that, he much preferred the accordion. It would make him smile today to know that we eventually worked the accordion into the band.

The Summer of Love and Fitness

That summer of 2012 was an idyllic one as I remember it. Daddy was maintaining his health, and with some gentle nudging, he started walking every afternoon. At first, I would go with him, but he preferred to go when he desired and at his own pace, and I think he enjoyed the time to himself. It was never a long walk, but it got him up and moving, and that was important.

I had allowed my weight to creep up once again, a lifelong pattern of mine, and I decided that if I was going to be a caregiver for Daddy, I needed to take better care of myself as well. I began a rigid diet and exercise regime, which often meant I prepared meals for Dad and Homer that I did not eat. After I served supper and called them to the table, I'd take a long bike ride. On occasions when dinner was late, Dad would remind me to wear my neon green safety vest and get home before dark. I would return to find Homer and Dad comfortably seated in their recliners watching TV together. Sometimes I could get a card game going, but often the evenings just gently wound down.

Homer worked most days, while Dad and I went about the business of daily life at home. Between cooking, cleaning, and exercising, I drove Dad to various appointments, band practice, square dancing, and church. I swung by the library weekly to keep him in books, which he continued to motor through. Often, he sat soaking up the sun in the glider on the porch, reading or watching or dozing. Mid-afternoon I could sometimes talk him into a bowl of popcorn or a piece of pie. He didn't talk much, and he didn't ask for much, but he didn't need to. We had settled into a comfortable, easy routine that suited us both, and the summer slipped away.

I was surprised and grateful that his kidneys were functioning as well as they were. His creatinine levels seemed to have hit a plateau. His appetite, bladder functions, and mobility were all good. No one would guess that in January this eighty-nine-year-old man had been given a six- month-to-a-year death sentence. Other than the usual aches and pains that accompany old age, he seemed to be the picture of good health. For me, this was more than I could have hoped for, and I was so very grateful. I think Homer, however, was quietly second-guessing the decision to have this old man move in with us and wondering just how long it would be until our lives returned to the normal we used to know.

FALL, WINTER, SPRING, SUMMER, AND FALL

Machtan family, Daddy's 90th birthday, November 2012

The Honeymoon is Over

In late September, Homer's friend Buckshot moved his portable sawmill to our place for the purpose of cutting into lumber some of the trees Homer had taken down. They set up towards the end of our long driveway, and I placed a lawn chair nearby so Dad could watch. This was the kind of thing Dad had often done himself when he was younger, and he enjoyed the distraction and conversation. One midafternoon I was on my way to the garden as he was headed to the house, and I said, "How's the supervising going?"

"Good," he said, "but I gotta go to the can," and he hobbled past me in what for him was a hurry.

I didn't think anything more about it until the next day when Homer came up the basement steps after putting a load of laundry in, grabbed me roughly by the arm and growled, "We need to take a walk."

His blue eyes were blazing, and I knew the answer before I even finished the question. "Is something wrong?" I asked.

"You're goddamned right something's wrong," he spit

out between gritted teeth. "I've been all smiles and patient with your old man since he moved in, but this just tears it."

"What..." I started, but he was on a roll.

"It's bad enough he only takes a bath once a week and stinks to high heaven. And no wonder. You know what I found when I was doin' his laundry just now? His pants and underwear covered in shit. In SHIT!!! He must have shit his pants, and instead of cleaning up after himself, he just put that goddamned mess in the bottom of the clothes basket and covered it up with other clothes, like some little kid hiding a toy he broke. What a fucking mess! That's what I have to deal with when I'm doing HIS laundry. Jesus Christ!" he fumed.

"Oh geez," I murmured. "That must have been yesterday when he was hurrying to the bathroom. I guess he waited too long and couldn't make it."

"I don't give a goddamn when it happened. He should have dealt with it himself. He didn't even take a shower afterwards or rinse out his clothes, much less wash them, the goddamn slob. Just hid it like no one would ever notice, expecting me to deal with it. I didn't agree to him living with us so I could be his damn slave. He doesn't pay a nickel's worth of rent, hasn't even offered, doesn't buy groceries, doesn't share utilities, never buys dinner when we go out...nothing. The most he does is pay for gas once in a while, and that's not often enough. I've been a nice guy up until now. Every day no matter how irritating he is, I grin and bear it. Well, I'm done with that. I will NEVER deal with something like this again. Either you talk to him, or I will. And I want him to start paying his way. He's going to pay $400 a month rent, or he's going to get out. It would cost him a hell of a lot more than that to be in assisted living, and he can afford it. He's been living off us for nine months already. He's always bragging about how much money he's got in savings; let the stingy old bastard spend some of it."

My heart sank. "I'm sorry, Homer," I said quietly. "You shouldn't have had to deal with any of this. I'll take over laundry. I'll talk to him about what happened. And I'll ask him about the rent."

"No," Homer insisted. "You'll TELL him about the rent. And I'll keep doing laundry, so I'll KNOW if it ever happens again. And it better not. For Christ's sake, he's an old man, not a baby."

"Sometimes there's not much difference," I said. "I'm sure he didn't do this on purpose. He just lost control. It can happen."

"Of course it can happen," Homer said, somewhat mollified. "It's happened to me. But when it does, I handle it; I don't ignore it. If I'm gonna clean up shit, I expect to get paid for it."

"He was embarrassed and humiliated," I speculated. "I bet he was too ashamed to say anything at all."

"Well, he's gonna have to get over it," Homer concluded, "because we both know this is only going to get worse. It's time for you two to have a heart-to-heart. If you don't do it, I will. And while you're at it, tell him he's going to start taking a bath twice a week. Whether he likes it or not."

"I'll do it," I reluctantly agreed. "But it's going to be horrible."

"Not as horrible as the shit in the laundry basket," Homer muttered. "Deal with it."

We walked back to the house in silence, me miserable about what had happened and the upcoming conversation, Homer still fuming but gradually getting himself under control. His resentment had clearly been building all summer, so when he finally lost it, he lost it big-time. He remained in the garage while I went in to the house, steeling myself for what was going to be a very difficult talk with my dad. How to even begin?

"Dad," I said. "I need to talk to you. Did you lose control of your bowels yesterday?"

Dad didn't look up from his book. "Yeah," he muttered. "I was out at the sawmill operation, and I had to go, but I didn't make it to the bathroom in time."

"That can happen," I said. "What did you do with your dirty clothes?"

"Put 'em in the clothes basket," he said.

"Did you rinse them out first? Then take a shower?" I probed.

"Nah," he said, eyes still fixed on the page.

"Daddy," I gently said as I sat next to him, closed the book, and took his hand. "I know that had to be awful for you. How often does this happen?"

"Not much," Dad said. "Maybe once or twice a year. Usually I can get to the toilet in time."

"I get that, Daddy," I said. "But when something like this happens, you've got to tell me about it. You can't just ignore it. You left a big mess for Homer to deal with, and he shouldn't have to do that."

"Yeah, I know," Dad muttered.

"So," I said, "if this happens again, you just tell me, and we'll get you cleaned up and deal with the dirty clothes. Are you OK with that?"

"Yup," he said, and turned back to his book.

Now or never, I reminded myself. "And there's another thing, Dad," I said. You've been here almost nine months, and you're doing great. Your health is good, and we're happy about that. But we are noticing quite a few expenses connected with having you here that we didn't expect. Do you think you would be willing to pay rent?"

"Sure," he said. "How much you want?"

"Well, how does $400 a month sound?" I answered. "Does that seem fair?"

"If it works for you, it works for me," he said. "Want to start the first of October?"

"That would be great," I said, saying a silent prayer of thanks that this had gone so well. One more hurdle. "And since you're going to be paying all that money, I want you to get more bang for your buck. Take another bath in the middle of the week. One on Tuesday or Wednesday, and another on Sunday night. Can you do that?"

"I don't think that's necessary," Dad said.

"But I do," I concluded. "Sometimes you have body odor. Nobody wants that. Is it a deal?"

"Oh, all right," he conceded.

"You know I love you, don't you, Daddy? And that I'm glad you're here?"

"Sure, Kid," he nodded. And then he turned back to his book, the changes were made, and we never spoke of it again.

Taking a Break--Almost

By October Homer and I needed some time away. Dad had been living with us since January, and while I was frequently gone from home doing my consulting work, Homer hadn't been anywhere, and we hadn't carved any time out at all for just the two of us. Day-to-day work responsibilities along with Dad's care were taking their toll on us, and I thought Dad might need a break as well. I knew that Sue would check in on Dad from time to time, but I was a little uneasy about leaving him home alone, and probably feeling a little guilty besides, so I called Ken and asked him if he would drive north to spend a long weekend with Dad. Daddy, of course, said that was completely unnecessary, but I told him I wanted to try to talk Ken into painting the bathroom while he was there, so Dad let it go. I thought it also would be good for Dad and Ken to spend some time together. They had never been close, and this would at least put them in the same place for more than just a few hours. And, to be honest, I thought it might give Ken more of an appreciation for our decision to take Dad in. Ken didn't hesitate when I asked him to do it, so all we needed now was a destination.

We had never been to Mackinac Island, a popular tourist destination about five and a half hours away, and since it was October and fall colors were peaking, it was a great time of year for the drive. Homer made reservations at a lovely hotel, and we spent the long weekend wandering the island, eating, drinking, and remembering why we got married in the first place. Despite cool temperatures and pounding rain, for the most part, it was an idyllic getaway.

Still, through no fault of his own, Dad managed to intrude. There was plenty of privacy for conversation, and I soon learned that Homer was still not satisfied with the economic arrangements we had settled on for Dad. It was becoming obvious since Dad's health had stabilized that we would be caring for Dad not for six months as we had originally imagined, but well into the future. Homer was facing this indefinite period of living as a threesome with trepidation and resentment, particularly toward my brothers who up until now had offered little or no help. He knew Dad's will specified a four-way equal division of his assets, but Homer wanted us to be compensated for the $4000 a month that Dad would otherwise be paying for an assisted living facility. I understood his position but told him that money had not been my motivation when I invited Dad to live with us, and it shouldn't be a factor now. "That's all well and good," Homer said. "But the fact is, this is turning into a much bigger deal than we thought it was going to be. It is fundamentally unfair and wrong that Ken, Dale, and Marti will receive an equal share of his inheritance when they've done nothing for him other than carry his name. In the past ten months, we've probably saved him $40,000, and he's paid us $400. That's not right."

"What exactly do you want me to do about this?" I demanded.

"Talk to him about changing his will," he said.

"Oh, for God's sake, I'm not going to tell him to cut the rest of the family out of the will!!" I exploded.

"That's not what I'm saying," Homer countered. "His will needs to be revised anyway since he's no longer married. I think he should add a line that says an additional amount should be paid to us for every month he lives with us."

"He might just as well be in assisted living then," I countered.

"I'm not saying it should be $4000 a month, but if it were half that, it would at least be a reasonable payment for turning our lives upside down the way we have."

"This is my dad, not some guy off the street," I said. "We should have talked about all of this before he ever moved in."

"You're right," Homer agreed. "But we didn't. We didn't see what was coming. But now we do. And this isn't just about you. This is affecting every day of my life too. I like your dad, but he's hard to live with. I didn't marry him. I married you. We don't know how long he's going to live, but it's clear that he's not going to die any time soon. This could go on for years. It's only fair that we're compensated for what we're doing."

"I'll think about it," I said. "But I don't want to talk about this anymore this weekend. It breaks my heart to even contemplate a conversation like this with my dad. You've said what you have to say. I've listened. We'll talk about it again after I've had time to think about it."

"All right," Homer conceded, "but I'm not going to wait forever. This needs to be taken care of." And although we didn't talk about it anymore that weekend, it weighed heavily on my mind. The heartburn I had been experiencing intermittently while dieting all summer returned with a vengeance, both literally and figuratively, for the rest of the weekend.

We returned home three days later, relatively refreshed and laden with four kinds of fudge for Ken and Dad. My bathroom had a fresh coat of paint, and Dad had been well-fed throughout the weekend. Ken left immediately after we returned, and when we talked on the phone later, I asked him how it had gone. "Well," he said, "it was OK, but he sure doesn't say much. It was almost like I was there by myself, except he was always sitting in that chair in the living room. It's almost spooky."

"Yup," I said. "Welcome to my world. Did he say anything about how he feels about living with us?"

"Oh yeah," Ken said. "He says you guys are great, and that Homer is a prince of a guy. He seems really happy."

"That's wonderful," I thought to myself. "If only Homer were happy too."

Our conversation about the will weighed heavily on me. I tried to see things from everyone's point of view. I knew there was legitimacy to what Homer said, but I also hated having him telling me what to do. I had no intention of asking Dad for additional money while he was alive. He had worked hard his entire life and saved for his old age. If he lived long enough, his money would run out, there would be no inheritance to split, and the issue would be moot. On the other hand, I, too, took umbrage at equal distribution of what might be left over, and I also knew that Dad's needs were going to become increasingly demanding over time. Eventually I would be unable to leave him alone, and that would be the end of my working, which would clearly become a financial burden for us. I conducted these mental debates day and night, and I knew I wouldn't sleep until I made a decision.

Finally, I reached a compromise. I decided I would talk to Dad and explain our position. I would ask him to update his will, including a provision for me to receive an additional $2000 for every month he lived with us starting in January of the coming year. That would mean we'd receive nothing other than three months' rent for the first year. I knew that wouldn't completely satisfy Homer, but it made me feel better. A year took into account the amount of time we had expected to be caring for Dad when we originally offered, and it reflected the fact that I hadn't made that decision to profit from the situation. On the other hand, it was fair compensation for his continued care.

I dreaded bringing any of this up to Dad, and I did not tell Homer what I had decided. This was between Daddy and me, no one else. The conversation went better than I expected, especially since I learned Dad had already been thinking about his will. "I don't think it's quite fair," he said. "Not about the way it's divided between you and Ken and Dale, but about Marti. Your mom said he should get Glenn's share, even though we agreed Cliff's kids were not going to be included. We both knew they'd just piss it away. But Glenn never had any use for me, and Marti doesn't seem to either. I'm not sure he should get anything."

"Well, that's up to you, Daddy," I said. "Why don't you think about this for a while, and we'll talk about it when you're ready?"

"No," Dad said. "It's the way your mom wanted it. She never expected Glenn would die before we did, and that Marti would get his share, but I'm not going against her wishes. Just have the lawyer change it the way you said, and we'll leave it at that."

A few days later I asked him if he was still satisfied with that decision, and he said he was and that I should go ahead and contact the attorney. I did so. It wasn't until after I made the phone call that I told Homer what we had decided. I know he wasn't delighted with the compromise, but he said he could at least live with it. And I could live with myself. I hoped that this would curb Homer's resentment. It did. For a while.

Celebrating Ninety Years

Dad was turning ninety on November 8, 2012. I had been thinking all summer about this milestone, and I wanted him to have a big party. I also knew it was up to me to make it happen. I ran the idea past Dale and Ken and they basically said, "Just tell us when to show up." I had organized a surprise party for his 80th birthday, but that one only involved the Noelder and Machtan families. I wanted this one to be open to absolutely everyone important to Dad. That meant he needed to have input on the guest list, so keeping this a surprise was out of the question. Together we chose the date, venue, and guests, and then I did the rest. He was very much looking forward to this event, and I intended to pull out all the stops.

To encourage as many people as possible to attend, we selected the same Marshfield supper club I had used for Dad's 80th. This time his party would be on a Sunday, so we settled on a brunch. The cost was reasonable, and since people would pay for their own meals, there was no need to limit the guest lists, only the need for RSVPs. It is a sad fact of life that most 90-year-olds outlive many of their friends and relatives, so I wasn't sure what kind of turnout to expect. When the RSVPs started to come in, it became apparent how well-loved Daddy was. All of Ruth's children, even those from out of the area, were attending, along with several grandchildren and great grandchildren. Immediate and extended family, neighbors, friends, and square dancers all said "yes." The only notable absence was Homer, whose annual fall hunting trip out West fell at the same time. My dad was OK with that. In his younger days, if he had had to choose between hunting and a party, hunting would have won hands down.

 I had asked Dale's family to help with the decorating, and they did a fine job. By the time Dad and I arrived, the banquet room was looking quite festive. I pinned a boutonniere on Dad's suit jacket, took a few pictures, and sent him on his way to greet his guests. When everyone was assembled, Ruth's son Richard offered a prayer, people helped themselves to an ample brunch buffet, and the conversation buzzed. After the meal, the program I had organized began. Two of Dale's grandsons, Soren and Magnus, played a happy birthday duet on keyboard and guitar. Richard and Dee did a costumed rendition of "There's a Hole in the Bucket, Dear Liza." I showed a PowerPoint of pictures of Dad's entire life set to "What a Wonderful World" by Louis Armstrong and "I'm Alive" by Kenny Chesney and Dave Matthews. Photo after photo of ninety years of farming, hunting, fishing, dancing, and family floated past. The last slide read "The End—Not Yet!" I had spent hours on it, and I was so pleased to see lots of smiles and tears as people viewed it. Speeches were spoken. Glasses were raised. Cameras flashed. Cake was cut. "Happy Birthday" was sung. I wandered out to the buffet area to check with the serving staff about how the brunch checks should be handled, only to be told that Marti had picked up the entire cost of everyone's meal. "Really????" I said. "Yes, really," the manager answered. The guests were shocked and delighted when I announced that Marti had picked up the tab, as was Daddy. Such a generous thing for him to do. Suddenly I was feeling wonderful about Dad's decision regarding the will.

Eventually people said their goodbyes, and we were left to take down the decorations, distribute leftover cake, pack up the cards and gifts, and head home. As we got in the car and started back north, Daddy said, "Kid, that was a great party. What a turnout! I know this took a lot of work. Thank you."

"You're welcome," I said. "Did you ever figure you'd make it to ninety?"

"I thought it might happen," Daddy said in his usual understated way. "But you just never know. One thing's for sure. I won't turn ninety again." When he was right, he was right. I was glad that I had made this one count.

Settling in to Change

Thanksgiving followed the big birthday bash. We had been invited by the Noeldners for their celebration, and Daddy was delighted to spend the day with Ruth's family. It was obvious how much he had missed them. Everyone was surprised that Daddy wasn't deer hunting, something he had loved and lived for since he was a teenager and continued to do even after he married Ruth. He didn't complain about his decision to hang up his rifle, but deer season in Northern Wisconsin takes on a life of its own, and I knew that he was missing his time in the woods. Still, he seemed to enjoy the Noeldner hunting stories, as well as being surrounded by his second family whom he had previously joined for so many dinners and celebrations.

November gave way to December Christmas preparations. We were hosting so that Dad wouldn't have to travel, and he benefited all month from the extra Christmas cookie baking and candy making. As usual, I gave him his own stash of homemade chocolate covered cherries, which he rationed out one a day as if they were the last ones that would ever grace the face of the earth. And as usual, he sent me on a buying mission from which I returned with a shopping cart overflowing with boxes and boxes of Zachary assorted chocolates for his Christmas gift-giving. We made a run to Marshfield in December for square-dancing and a visit to Ruth's kids, where we dropped off his traditional presents. Throughout the month, he received a few Christmas cards, enjoyed our towering tree, and looked forward to the family gathering in our Rhinelander home, but it was clearly not the Christmas he had grown accustomed to in the last ten years. Still, I did my best to make it festive, and the candlelight Christmas Eve service we attended was probably the highlight.

Christmas Day the caravan of family pulled in all at once in a burst of cold air, noise, and confusion. It was the first time most of them had been to our house since Dad moved in eleven months earlier, even though we lived only a hundred miles away. They stayed a few hours, played cards, chatted and ate, and after dinner roared off again for the trip home. After all the noise of twenty-some adults and kids, the subsequent silence was almost deafening. And welcome. At least for a while. Winter had officially settled in, and it would be a long, cold, quiet time before the next family gathering at Easter.

Time for a Break

As the winter of 2013 dragged on, my friend Terri and I were going stir crazy. When I broached the idea of a trip to Florida, Homer wasn't delighted with Dad-sitting for a week, but he knew I'd been working hard and could use a break from the snow and cold. Terri and I had a nice time visiting our friend Sarah, but by the time we returned home, Rhinelander had had another major blizzard. Homer and Dad, along with everyone else, were socked in again, and my return didn't come any time too soon for them. They were getting on each other's nerves, both were sick of Homer's cooking, and although neither of them said anything to me, I think they each were pretty resentful about my absence. I know I would have been.

Homer said he was ready for a break as well, and so we booked a flight to Scotland at the end of May. Ken agreed to stay with Dad and the dogs, and we headed out, just the two of us, for our first vacation since Mackinac Island. It was high time. We had a wonderful trip, with no schedule to maintain, no work, no Dad, just a total escape from reality. I didn't feel too guilty about Dad being alone, because I knew he was in good hands with Ken. We refer to that trip as Homer's Whiskey Tour. He sampled whiskey from any number of distilleries and pubs, and for a while we both forgot about being caregivers. By now Daddy had been living with us for sixteen months, and he showed no significant signs of decline. While that made me very happy, it begged the question: how much longer would we be responsible for his well-being? Six months had turned to twelve, then turned to sixteen, and there was no end in sight. I was very grateful for this reprieve, but Homer could only see an endless future of caregiving and inconvenience with a staggering loss of freedom and privacy. I am glad now that I didn't and couldn't see what was coming.

It All Depends

The summer of 2013 marked Dad's steady but slow decline, and every month seemed to present new challenges. Dad's omnipresent body odor was due to both a continued reluctance to bathe and the toxins his body was steadily producing. Homer began a passive-aggressive campaign against the smell regardless of Daddy's complaints of being too cold by constantly opening windows. I would sneak behind Homer and close them, trying to be unnoticed, but an hour or so later, Homer would open them again. Dad would mutter under his breath about Homer opening the damned windows, and Homer would complain to me about the need for fresh air every time he found them closed again.

It was about a month later when Homer noticed Dad's underwear, which he didn't change nearly enough, was also often urine soaked. The incontinence the doctors had predicted had finally presented itself, and its frequency was steadily increasing. I found myself again in the awkward position of having to discuss this with my dad, along with his need for Depends. He didn't want to admit he needed them, but I bought them anyway, trying to figure out the right size and absorbency. At first, they were falling off him because he was so skinny. When I finally got the size right, they were falling off because he refused to change them more than once a day, and they would be so soaked with urine that his jeans would be damp. Homer would report seeing him going from bathroom to bedroom with the sodden adult diapers hanging around his knees. "They are soaked with piss," Homer growled. "Why the fuck doesn't he put on dry ones?" I wondered the same thing, but I suspected it was because they were expensive, so he didn't want to change them more than absolutely necessary. The baths didn't increase, the body odor did, and the battle of the windows continued well into fall. Despite numerous attempts to discuss the need for frequent changes, Daddy hated admitting he had been reduced to wearing adult diapers, and he refused to acknowledge it even when confronted. It didn't matter how many packages of Depends were on hand, or how cleverly I shopped for bargains, it continued to be an issue.

An additional change for the worse was Dad's inability to put on his own socks and shoes. He simply didn't have the flexibility to bend in the way necessary to get them on. Each morning he would sit on the steps leading to the loft and wait for me to wrestle him into his tube socks and oxfords. It was a task neither of us enjoyed–him because he hated needing help, and me because I was so clumsy in my efforts.

Daddy was also becoming less and less stable on his feet. It was clear to everyone but him that the cane he had come to depend upon was inadequate. I worried about him taking walks alone with only a cane for support, but I also knew that he needed the exercise. I suggested we get a walker, but he didn't want one. It would be a cumbersome constant reminder of his frailty, and he wasn't ready for that. "Walkers are for old people," he groused, and he clearly wasn't one of them.

We compromised on a Life Alert system, so that at least he could get help if he fell and was alone. He also argued that it wasn't necessary, but I pointed out that with both

Homer and me working, he was alone too much to have no emergency system at all, and if he wasn't going to use a walker, he at least needed some way to get help. I guess he thought it was easier to agree with me than listen to my nagging, so we ordered it, and he wore it all the time.

It wasn't long after that when my dad fell while walking into church. A young boy was politely holding the door open for him. Somehow Daddy's cane got tangled up between the boy's feet and the door, and down Dad went. I could see it unfolding but was helpless to prevent the fall. Although only his pride was hurt, it scared me to death. Two of the ushers helped him up, eased him into a wheelchair, and gently said, "LaVerne, you might want to consider a walker. Other people in the church use one." That's all I needed to hear to make up my mind that relying on a cane was no longer negotiable. On Monday we drove together to the medical supply store and picked out a shiny new red walker with a seat he could use if he tired when he was out and about. He didn't like it much. He didn't want to use it. But I could be just as stubborn as he was. Eventually the walker replaced his cane whenever he was outdoors, and that gave me a certain amount of peace of mind.

The final attempt to make him comfortable and increase his ease of mobility involved replacing his ratty old recliner. It had been worn out and disgusting when he brought it with him from Spencer, and we would have much preferred that he left it there. But he was insistent that it had a lot of wear left in it. A year and a half later, it smelled and looked even worse, but more importantly, he had to struggle to get in and out of it. Ruth had had a lift chair when they were married, and he knew how much easier it had made life for her. I found a gently used one advertised for sale and suggested we look at it. Surprisingly, he was willing, so we took a long drive to hunt it down, and by the end of the day he was the proud owner of a state of the art, pristine lift chair. It took up a lot more space in our little living room, but Homer was delighted to haul the old stinky recliner out to the front yard and set it ablaze. Still, he had to say to me as we watched it burn, "I wonder how long until the new one is just as raunchy as that one was."

    It seemed the more I tried to troubleshoot the issues Daddy was having, the more trouble there was to shoot. I suppose I knew it was a losing battle, both with my father and my husband, but I just kept buying ammunition and loading the guns.

Point of No Return

Summer started to turn to fall. Early September arrived, and with it increased consulting gigs. I was working for five Wisconsin schools by then, ranging from Land O'Lakes in the far north to Albany, close to the Illinois border. I was making good money and enjoying the work immensely, but I was away from home more than ever, leaving Homer responsible for Daddy's care, and Homer wanted no part of it. By then he had come to resent my father's constant presence. It wasn't so much that Daddy was demanding; it was that he was still *there*, an unwelcome guest who had long overstayed Mark Twain's three-day visitor and fish rule. Homer no longer thought or referred to him as LaVerne, just "that old man." Each time I returned after two or three days of consulting, Homer had a long list of grievances to air privately with me. When I left the next time, I dreaded what might happen while I was gone, and what I would face upon my return. "He can't stay here forever," was Homer's constant refrain, but I couldn't bear the thought of asking my dad to leave. "We can do this," I would say. But the truth was, Homer was doing most of it, he no longer wanted to, and I didn't think that I could do it all by myself.

On my long car rides around the state, I sorted through options. Maybe it would just work itself out, I hoped. Maybe Homer would suddenly become more patient and forgiving. Or maybe Dad would recognize what was happening and decide it was time to move. Maybe my brothers would step up and one of them would open their homes to our father. That, I was sure, had never crossed their minds, or Dad's. All these options were completely out of the question. I also knew Dad would never want to move into assisted living, but that my marriage could not withstand much longer the tension of the three of us living together. Maybe Daddy and I should both move out and rent an apartment, just the two of us, so that I could continue to provide the home I had offered him. But who would look after him when I was away from home working, how could I alone take care of him when his health declined, and was this financially feasible? More importantly, was I willing to choose between my father or my husband? These thoughts went 'round and 'round in my head both day and night, eating me alive, but no solution seemed viable. I kept all of this bottled up inside, ashamed to tell my father, friends, and family of the coming storm and too afraid of what a no-holds barred discussion with Homer would bring. So instead I said nothing, hoping to delay the day of reckoning.

In some ways the biggest decisions are prompted by the smallest, most innocuous things. One evening after supper Homer was reading the newspaper, Dad was sitting in his recliner, and I was cleaning up the kitchen. "I think I might take some time off from logging and trap again this fall," Homer announced. "Fur prices are high, so I could make some money at it."

It had been years since he had trapped, but this was a shared interest for him and my dad, who had also trapped his entire adult life. When I first started dating Homer, they had spent a lot of time swapping trapping stories and tips, and my dad immediately took a liking to this young man so similar to himself. I thought that this resurgence in a mutual hobby might go a long way towards keeping the peace.

But I was so very, very wrong. Even though Daddy hadn't said anything up until now, he too must have felt Homer's growing resentment over the past months, and apparently, he decided to vent his own anger. As Homer was rattling off the prices he believed muskrat, beaver, fox, and mink were likely to bring, Dad scoffed and said, "Yeah, right. What makes you think you're gonna be able to get that kind of money for fur? You're dreaming." The conversation ended right there. Homer got up, walked upstairs to his desk, and said no more the rest of the night until he came to bed. But then he had plenty to say.

"That's it," he fumed. "Nobody calls me stupid in my own home, especially that old man. I read. I listen to the news. I'm smarter and better informed than he ever was or will be, and I know what fur prices are going to be. I'm sick to death of him and his smug, know-it-all-attitude. I've put up with him twice as long as he was supposed to be here. He's no longer welcome, and I want him out."

"Oh, for God's sake, Homer," I said. "It was just an off-hand remark. You're making a mountain out of a mole hill."

"No, I'm not," he said through gritted teeth. "I'm done with him. By the time I get home after hunting in Wyoming in early November, he's either gone, or I'm throwing him out."

"I get it. You're angry right now, and you feel like he challenged you. He didn't mean anything. Just let it go, and sleep on it. You'll feel differently in the morning," I said.

"No, I won't. This has been coming for a long time. I did my part. It was supposed to be six months to a year, not a life sentence. I've done his laundry. Hauled him everywhere he wants to go. Cooked his meals. Disposed of his diapers. Put up with his stinking. Put up with his television. Put up with every other damned thing. I'm finished. He goes. We're done talking. Make it happen."

YEAR TWO

Finding Grace

We didn't speak about it the next morning. In fact, we didn't speak any more about it at all. It was late September by then, and I knew that talking and thinking about Dad's moving were no longer enough. It was time to explore options and decide.

I was very familiar with two of the assisted living centers in Rhinelander. Both had housed elderly friends of mine, and both seemed reasonable places to start. I stopped first at the facility where my dear friend Kitty had lived for over a year. I had visited her every week with my Westie Willie. Even as her health declined, she received excellent care from an attentive, sympathetic staff. I was sitting with her at her bedside, singing softly and listening to her shallow and slowing breathing the morning she died. I hadn't been back since.

The place had been sold and was under different management, and I suspected much had changed. When I parked my car and walked in, an old gentleman whom I didn't recognize smiled and said, "We've been waiting for you. Where is your little white dog?" It had been nine years since I last was there, and it seemed impossible that any of the residents I once knew could still be living. It must be weird coincidence, I thought, or maybe, just maybe, a sign from Kitty that this place was waiting to welcome me back, this time with my dad.

As I made my way to the manager's office, my initial first positive impression disappeared. The place was dark, aging, and almost empty of staff. Residents seemed detached, disengaged, and barely functioning. This was no place for my father. Still, I knocked on the office door, introduced myself, and explained my circumstances, as much, at least, as I could bear to share with this stranger. I asked all the questions I had prepared regarding services, cost, and availability. Astutely, the manager asked, "This seems to have come on suddenly. Why the hurry? And why isn't your father visiting with you today?" Too ashamed to speak the truth, I mumbled some garbage about my busy work schedule and the need for my dad to be surrounded by more people. I didn't think she bought it, and I didn't care. I had already decided I would rent an apartment for Daddy and me before I would have him move to this dismal place for the dying. Very little living seemed to be assisted here.

Fighting back tears as I left, I drove to Grace Lodge. My friend Jane's parents had both lived here for several years, and a few years before I retired, I had initiated an "Adopt a Grandparent" program between my students and the residents. Every month we walked from our school to their building to socialize. Willie went with us, and he was just as popular as the students with the residents and staff. As time passed, I got to know both the activities director, Brenda, and the manager, Maureen, quite well. Sometimes I played my accordion for the residents' weekly cocktail hour.

I parked my car in front of a large stone that had been beautifully engraved with a dove and the words Grace Lodge. It read, "My grace is sufficient for you, for my power is made perfect in weakness. 2 Cor. 12:9." I sat and looked at it for a long time, then finally took a deep breath and headed in. Inside the doors I was impressed as always by the elegance of this place. It was tastefully decorated, full of sparkling chandeliers, polished glass, plush carpeting, linen tablecloths, and comfortable upholstered furniture. There was nothing institutional or depressing about it. It looked like and was an upscale apartment complex. I made my way to Maureen's manager's office.

She smiled and said, "What brings you here today, Darlene? Not playing the accordion for us, are you?"

"Noooo," I reluctantly began. "I'm here about my dad." And then I burst into tears, the floodgates truly opening for the first time in months. Maureen had obviously been down this road before. She handed me a box of tissues, gently closed the door, and said, "OK, let's start at the beginning."

I told her the story of how Daddy had come to live with us, the journey until now, warts and all. I told her about his declining health, and how his renal disease was going to progress. I told her that he would be absolutely opposed to making this move, both personally and financially, and I told her that Homer and I had reached an impasse. She listened quietly and without judgement. She answered my questions and allayed many of my fears, especially when I asked her if Daddy would be able to remain there as his kidneys failed. She said that since he was still ambulatory, of sound mind, and in reasonably good health, he was eligible to move in, but more importantly to me, to also remain and be cared for until he died. "The only exception," she said, "is if he were to become aggressive or combative. Then you would have to find another place for him. Is that in his nature?"

I thought of my mild-mannered, easy-going dad and said, "Not in the least, but I guess you never know."

"Actually," Maureen said, "we kind of do. Most residents' personalities stay the same despite their illnesses, except for those with dementia, and since your dad has no signs of that, he'd probably do OK here. Let's take a tour."

I was familiar with most of the facility because I had spent so much time there, but now I was looking at it through a whole new lens as the possible future home of my dad. Maureen showed me apartments of varying sizes, each with its own handicapped accessible walk-in shower, a vast improvement over our tub at home. Each apartment had a small kitchen with a stove, refrigerator, sink, and cupboards, even though three meals a day were included in the monthly rent. Dad could continue to monitor his own meds, or that service could be provided. The last apartment she showed me was on the second floor and had a beautiful view of the expansive lawn, woods, and river just behind the building. Maureen said there were frequent wildlife sightings, including waterfowl, whitetails, and an occasional bear. There was a place for a bird feeder right outside the window. It was as close to living in our country home as Daddy was going to get. And best of all, despite the waiting list I had expected, this apartment was available.

I had much to think about. I gathered up the brochures and paperwork Maureen had put together for me, gratefully accepted her warm hug, and headed out the door. This was the place, I thought, as good as it was going to get. Now I just had to figure out how in the world to broach it with Dad.

Finding Words

I knew that this was going to be the most difficult conversation I had ever had with Dad. For several days, I thought about what to say without coming up with a plan, so I called together my advisory circle of seven women, The W(h)iners. At our usual Friday night haunt and over our usual wine, I explained the circumstances that had led up to this, and I confessed the enormous regret and guilt I was feeling. I even shared my desire to run away from home to an apartment with just my father and me. Karen, always the realist and whose father was in similar straits said, "That's no solution, Darlene. Ultimately you aren't going to be able to care for him. You're going to need help in a facility where he is surrounded 24/7 by trained staff. No matter how much you want to be there for him, you can't do this alone."

"But how do I tell him?" I wailed. "He is going to feel so betrayed, so hurt."

"Maybe that's how you feel," Jane gently said. "Maybe your father will be more forgiving with you than you are with yourself. He knows you love him. He knows you have his best interest at heart. My mom and dad didn't want to move to Grace Lodge either, but they were grateful that I would be near, staying in touch and watching out for them. It turned out to be the best solution. There is no better assisted living place anywhere. My home wouldn't have worked for them. Your house can't work much longer either. It's too bad Homer's forcing the issue, but it would have come to this eventually. We're daughters, not nurses. There's only so much we can do before we need some help from professionals."

"But he's still OK," I countered.

Julie weighed in. "That's why it's time to do this. Maureen told you LaVerne is only eligible to move into Grace Lodge while he's still healthy enough to be independent. I know you don't want to think about his eventual decline—none of us do—but that's the reality. And the clock is ticking. He's already beaten the odds he was given, but you know that his kidneys will eventually fail, and when they do, you aren't going to be able to care for him. If he's not at Grace Lodge, he'll end up in a place like my dad did—and as you know, my dad lasted exactly one day there. That's not what you want."

Each of the women who knew me so well offered their insight and support. They urged me to talk to Daddy and arrange a tour of the facility. And they agreed that I should leave Homer out of the conversation. They knew that this needed to be just between Daddy and me.

When I got home that evening, I followed Daddy into his bedroom, shut the door behind me, and said, "Daddy, we need to talk."

"Then talk, Kid," he said.

I don't remember much of what I said, only that I put it all in terms of me and only me—how anxious I was when I had to leave him alone to do my consulting, how his failing health concerned me, how I didn't know how I could cope with his inevitable decline. I told him about how nice Grace Lodge is, and how I wouldn't have to worry about him struggling up steps anymore and climbing over the tub to shower. I told him he would have plenty of company during the long winter he would otherwise be often alone. I assured him we would still go to church every Sunday, just as we always had, and that he could come and go as he pleased. I told him Grace Lodge welcomed dogs, so the girls could visit him as often as he liked. I told him I knew he could afford this, and that he had worked hard his entire life to provide for his old age, and I was grateful for that. I told him that this was as much for me as for him, and that above all, I loved him. By then the tears were coursing down my cheeks, and I fell silent, just as he had been during my monologue. He said nothing for several minutes. Finally, he conceded, "Maybe someday, but I'm fine right now."

My heart sank. This was the answer I had anticipated and dreaded. "That's what I'm worried about Daddy," I said gently. "We don't know how long that'll last, and we have only a small window of time to get you into this place. We can't wait to decide until you really need it."

"I'll think about it," he said.

And that, I knew, was as good as it was going to get.

For now.

Resolution

I let a week or so pass, still having said nothing to Homer about Dad. We pretended he had never issued his ultimatum, and that was fine with me. I already had enough stress to deal with, and I knew I was not going to receive the support I needed from him. Once again, I turned to my women. Julie had known my parents for over twenty years, long before my mother died. She had visited them several times in Marshfield, and after Dad moved to Rhinelander, she came to our house regularly to chat and play cards. They had a mutual appreciation for each other's straightforwardness and senses of humor, and I knew Daddy valued her opinion. Jane also had spent time with my father, but more importantly, since her parents had lived at Grace Lodge for several years, she was my resident expert on assisted living and the heartache of care for aging parents. I asked the two of them if they would be willing to go with Daddy and me on a Grace Lodge field trip, during which they would gently but firmly voice support for the move. They didn't hesitate, so I called Maureen to arrange for a tour. I told Daddy that even though he didn't think a move was in order, I wanted him to at least see the place before he made up his mind. He was less than enthusiastic about the idea, but when he heard Julie and Jane would be joining us, he agreed.

Daddy took an immediate liking to Maureen, even though he assured her he was just fine living with me. "It doesn't hurt to have a look," she offered as she led us throughout the building. Every time we stopped, Julie and Jane commented on the amenities and advantages of living there. "This is way nicer than my house and most hotels I've stayed in, LaVerne," Julie said. "What's not to love? I'm inclined to move in here with you."

"And the food's great too," Jane attested. "My mom and dad really enjoyed it, but they also came to my house, or we went to restaurants sometimes, just to keep things interesting. Having your own kitchen comes in handy when you have company."

"Sounds like you'll eat better here than you do at Darlene's," Julie dryly added. "At least Grace Lodge gives you three squares a day, and you won't get stuck with Homer's famous beans or Spam dinner entrees when she's away from home." Julie knew that would speak to him.

Jane continued the sales pitch. "There's always recreation going on, musical groups coming in, lots to do. People play cards, bingo—there's a different activity scheduled every day. My folks really liked the social part of it, but when they wanted to be alone, they had all the privacy they wanted just by shutting the door."

"True," Julie said, "but LaVerne likes the outdoors. Look at these grounds—they are gorgeous. You can get outside and walk as much as you like, or just sit and soak up the sun."

"Never thought much of living in town," Dad muttered.

"This isn't all that different from living in Spencer," I countered. "It's on the edge of town, nestled back in all these trees and along the river. You can even fish if you want to."

"Some of our residents do," agreed Maureen. "There's a pier right over there. Sometimes we take pontoon rides in the summer too, or bus trips to community events. There's always something to do. Darlene said you like to read, so let me show you our library. We also have a Rhinelander district librarian who comes in to bring you any books you'd like if you don't want to go get them, but we encourage you to be as independent as possible. You're welcome to have a car here and drive yourself wherever you'd like."

"Nope, no drivin' for me anymore," Daddy said. "Darlene's my chauffeur."

"Well, that's certainly up to you," Maureen said, "but if you change your mind, you do have the option. Now, there's one apartment in particular I'd like to show you. Based on everything you said, I think you'll really like this one." We walked down the hall and into the single bedroom unit I had looked at on my previous visit. The view of the autumn foliage and the river behind it was stunning. The sun was shining brightly on the shimmering water, providing a tremendous sense of peace, security, and contentment. It seemed a good place to live, I thought, and yes, even a good place to die.

"Wow," Julie said. "What a view! This is gorgeous!! What do you think, LaVerne?"

"It's real pretty," he admitted. "But where's the furniture?"

"That we let you bring in," said Maureen, "although we do have a few pieces in storage you can use if you'd like."

"This apartment must be really popular," I said. "I bet there's a long, long waiting list."

"Normally you'd be right," said Maureen, "but it just became available. We'll be doing some cleaning and painting in the next couple of weeks, and then we'll rent it. If you want it, you can have it in early November. But I wouldn't wait too long to decide. This one will go especially fast, and the single bedroom apartments in general are harder to come by. Just let me know what you decide to do. Any questions?"

"How much?" Daddy asked.

"That depends on the level of care you want," Maureen said, "but I'd guess somewhere around $3000 a month. That includes your room, heat, electricity, television, meals, cleaning service, nursing care, emergency call button—everything but your phone, personal incidentals, and meds."

"That's a lotta money," Dad said.

"That's a lot of care," Jane pointed out. "My mom and dad checked out a half dozen places in Rhinelander before they moved in here. This was by far the best value. I think you'll see that if you shop around. I'm surprised you're even able to get in. That's really lucky."

"Plus, there's no lease," Maureen said. "You decide month-to-month whether or not this is the right place for you. You are always free to leave. But this isn't something you should decide right now. Talk it over, think about it, and when you make up your mind, just let me know."

We walked back downstairs, Julie, Jane, Maureen, and I chatting excitedly, Daddy saying nothing. As he started out to the car ahead of us, the three women turned to me, Jane nodded towards my dad, and then softly asked, "Well, what do you think?"

"I think this is the perfect place for him," I said, "and we maybe made a little headway here, but he's cheap as hell, and he doesn't want to move. I don't know what will happen."

"He's not going to do it for himself," Julie predicted. "He's going to do it for you. Just you wait and see."

Daddy and I spoke little on the way home. I knew he was thinking about it. That was enough. Later that afternoon, while I was bustling around the kitchen, he called me into his room. Without preamble he said, "So when do you want to move me to the home?"

I immediately started crying. "Oh, Daddy," I confessed. "I don't want to move you anywhere. I love you so much.

I wish you could stay here forever. But it's getting harder and harder, and I am on the road working more and more. I worry about you all the time. I'm afraid you'll fall, I'm afraid you'll get sick, I'm afraid of everything. It's not good for you to be alone so much of the time. When you first moved in, I was retired, but I'm gone half the time now. I like the work, and the money is great, but you need to have people around you—not be stuck out here in the country by yourself. It scares me to death. I know you think Grace Lodge is expensive. But it's your money. You've been frugal all your life. It's time to spend some of it on yourself."

Daddy said, "Don't cry, kid. You worry too much. But if moving to the home is what it's going to take to make you feel better, then I'll do it. I don't like it. But I'll do it. We'll figure out the rest later. Now go fix some supper."

Preparations

Dad and I went back and talked to Maureen shortly after Daddy agreed to move. I still felt terrible about forcing the issue, but I also didn't want to allow time for Dad to change his mind. The apartment with the good view would be available the first week of November, and that would allow me enough time to get it furnished and ready for occupancy. Daddy would move in November 8, which ironically happened to be his birthday. Some present.

Maureen welcomed us warmly. "It's good to see you again, LaVerne," she said. "We've got some paperwork to take care of, and details to work out. Let's start with the most important question. What brings you to Grace Lodge?"

"Oh God," I thought. "What's he going to say?"

"Well," Dad said, "she's kicking me out."

That was the moment my heart broke into a billion little pieces. No matter how I had tried to sugarcoat it, that was the explanation, plain and simple.

"Wow, Daddy," I said, "go right for the jugular."

He chuckled. Then he said, "She thinks she can't take care of me anymore because she's gone all the time making big bucks doing her consultant work. I'm just fine, but if this makes her feel better, well, OK."

Saint Maureen said matter-of-factly, "She loves you,

LaVerne, so she wants what's best for you. I think this is a very good decision." Then she redirected us to filling out forms, explaining the details of assisted living daily life, and reassuring him that he would be happy there and, if not, could leave any time he liked. She took his picture and told him that it would be included in the 2014 Grace Lodge calendar. "So, what will be your first day with us?" she asked.

"Well," I said. "His birthday is Friday, November 8. How would that be?"

"Excellent!!" Maureen exclaimed. "That means you get to choose the menu, have guests join us for lunch, and we all sing to you! It only happens on birthdays, and this is a great way for everyone to get to know you!! That's perfect!!!" She chatted him up for a few more minutes, asking him his favorite foods, what he'd like on the menu, and whom he wanted to invite. It was clear that Maureen was very, very good at her job and that he was not the first resident she had dealt with who was moving in with more than a bit of reluctance. By the time we left, he seemed, if not pleased, at least accepting of this major change in his life. I would try to make the transition as seamless as possible.

I really don't remember when I told Homer that Daddy was moving to Grace Lodge. I don't even know what he said, other than he had moved Dad into our house, and someone else was going to have to move him out. He had a hunting trip planned for the first two weeks in November, and he had no intentions of changing it–I would just have to find someone else to help. He did agree to go with me to haul home a couple of used dressers, which he thought were completely unnecessary purchases, but that is as far as it went. I was so angry and disappointed with him and myself that I was glad to see him leave for Wyoming and equally glad to be doing this on my own. Dad simply sat on the fringes and watched, as usual, saying little or nothing.

My friend Tracey offered to lend me a spare twin bed, a desk, a small kitchen table, chairs, and a couple of lamps. She had almost single-handedly furnished and decorated the house Homer and I had lived in temporarily after fire destroyed our home in 2010. Tracey had been our next-door neighbor for years, and her mother also lived in Grace Lodge. Tracey knew from experience that it was a difficult adjustment, so she once again rushed to my rescue. "This stuff is just cluttering up my basement," she said. "No sense buying new furniture. You can use it as long as you like." I was so grateful for the offer.

I called my brother Dale and asked him to come north to help move furniture from Tracey's and my house into Grace Lodge, and he and his son Chris did. It was clear that he felt inconvenienced and put upon, but he did it. Within a few hours, we had muscled the furniture up the stairs and into the second-floor apartment, and Dale and Chris were on their way once again. It is strange, but I have no idea of where Daddy was while all this was taking place. It is as if he were suspended in space and time while I readied this new nest for him. I mostly remember feeling absolutely alone—despite the whirlwind of activity and friends around me. I was just so very, very sad.

I told Tracey that she was welcome to go in and out of the unlocked apartment whenever she wanted while I was getting it organized. She often stopped before or after visiting her mom to see how it was shaping up. She has a wonderful eye and a decorator's touch, and each time I came, I would see her contributions. She purchased dinnerware and flatware that my dad didn't want and would never use, but which she insisted he needed to have, just in case. She added tiny details of color and touches of home that I would never have considered. With Jane's help, I managed to hang Dad's favorite pictures and install a bird feeder outside his window. I gradually moved in linens, towels, toiletries, clothes and shoes, an armload at a time, and by the end of the week, everything Daddy would need was settled into Grace Lodge, apartment 210. Except him.

Happy 91st Birthday

November 8 my father turned ninety-one. His vision was failing, his hearing was failing, his legs were failing, his balance was failing, his kidneys were failing, and above all, his daughter was failing. As we drove away from the house that had been his home for almost two years, I felt miserable, and although he said nothing, I suspect he did too. But feelings were never something we talked about, so instead we commented on the weather, the landscape, the roads, anything but what was foremost in both our minds.

When we arrived and met with Maureen, she promptly attached a Grace Lodge lifeline to Daddy's wrist. "I already have this one," Daddy said gesturing to his pendant.

"You won't need that one anymore," Maureen said. "This one connects directly to our staff. If you need anything, you just press the button. We'll be there in a jiffy." It seemed to me that that was a sugar-coated way of saying, "You're in our house now." It was a little bit scary to surrender that last bit of control, but it was also a large part of what we were paying for.

After Dad signed some final paperwork, Maureen escorted us to Daddy's room. This was the first time he'd seen it furnished, and he seemed pleased, especially with the view outside his window just past the bird feeder. "Better get some seed in that," he ordered, so I immediately complied, realizing that he had accepted he was here for the long haul and would never be alone if he had finches and red-winged blackbirds perched just outside. Maureen said lunch would be ready shortly and excused herself. I bustled around his room, pretending to be productive in an effort to avoid meeting his eyes.

Fortunately, just then Julie and Jane knocked on his open door, calling out "Happy Birthday, LaVerne!" and presenting a bouquet of cheerful balloons. They gushed over his lovely room, how handsome he looked, and the milestone of a 91st birthday. They filled the room with cheer and chatter, and Daddy responded in kind. By the time we headed down to lunch, he was in good spirits. We joined him at the table to which he was assigned, surrounded by a few other Grace Lodge gentlemen residents. Like all assisted living facilities, the number of women vastly surpassed the number of men. Maureen had chosen men with good senses of humor for Dad's table, and he eventually came to look forward to their company. On this day, however, Dad was pleased to have his daughter and two of her best friends as his guests. He was grinning as Maureen introduced all of us, and then we dove into his selected lunch of pork chops, potatoes, salad, and veggies. It was delicious, and as we looked around the dining room with its bright white linen table cloths and napkins, gleaming china and sparkling chandeliers, Julie sighed, "Oh, LaVerne, you've got it made. Look at this place. It's spotless, elegant, the food is great, and you don't have to lift a finger. I want to move in here with you." Before Daddy could think of a reply, as the residents and staff began to sing Happy Birthday, his cake was served. It was pineapple upside down cake, as requested, the only cake Dad ever really liked. When he blew out the candles, I could only wonder what he wished for.

As the dishes were cleared, Julie and Jane said their goodbyes, and Dad and I went back upstairs to his room. By this time, he was tired. After making sure he knew how to work his TV, I said I'd be on my way but back in the morning to check on him. I gave him a kiss goodbye, feeling like Judas, and walked out the door, one of the hardest exits I have ever made. The day had gone as well as it possibly could, but I was crying as I drove away, and I was still crying when I stumbled through the front door of my empty house.

The First Weekend

The next morning, I arrived at Dad's room around 10. He was sitting in his recliner reading, showered, shaved, and dressed. I asked him how he was doing. "OK, I guess," was all he said.

"How was breakfast?" I probed.

"OK, I guess."

"How did you sleep?"

He sighed, put down his book, and looked at me. "Not worth a damn. Strange bed. Strange place. Strange noises. It was a long, rough night."

"Oh, Daddy," I said softly. "That's terrible. I'm so sorry. Sleeping has always been your specialty."

"Yup, I can normally sleep anywhere. Even when I was in the Army during the war, I could always sleep," he said. "But not last night."

"Is there anything I can do?" I asked.

"Nah, I'll just have to get used to it," he concluded.

"Well, I hope tonight is better," I said. "We've got church in the morning and then we're headed to Dale's cabin to celebrate your and Chris' birthdays. You need to be bright-eyed and bushy-tailed for all that. Are you looking forward to it?"

"Yeah, it'll be nice to see everyone. Haven't talked to anybody since Labor Day. They probably are gettin' ready for deer season," he said wistfully.

"Do you miss that?" I asked.

"I hunted for over seventy years," he said. "I miss it. But I had a good run. Just too old and blind to do it anymore. Still like to talk about it, though. Heard anything from your old man about how things are goin' in Wyoming?"

"Just an antelope, so far," I said. "But they have muley and elk tags to fill, so they're still at it. He'll be out there another week or so, I imagine."

"Hope they're havin' a great time," Daddy said. Despite the rancor that had developed on Homer's part, and despite that he'd done nothing to assist in the move, Daddy felt no ill will towards Homer. I wished that I could say the same. For now, I was grateful for his absence.

We chatted until it was time for lunch, while I tried to set up his new "simple" cell phone. I was having a terrible time following the directions, and I was glad that tomorrow I would have nephews and a niece with enough tech savvy to get it working. I walked him down to lunch, explaining that I had party favors to work on that afternoon. I told him that he would see the results the next day. I reminded him that I'd be picking him up for church at 9:45, and he assured me he'd be ready to roll.

When I got home, the house felt hollow and empty. It had been a long time since I had been there all alone, and I felt ill at ease and lonely. Despite cleaning and chores that should have taken precedence, I distracted myself by customizing labels for my homemade jam. I found a great picture of Dad and Chris in my pile of photo albums. I edited and scanned it and then designed the label. After experimenting with various wording, fonts, sizes, and placement, I finally settled on a template, with "Well Preserved," their names, and birth dates typed below the photo. I printed the labels, placed them on a variety of jams and jellies, boxed them up, and put them in the car for the following day. I knew that nobody but me would probably even notice or care about the effort that went into this, but it was a welcome change from focusing on the move.

The next morning, I picked Daddy up for church. He was all dressed up in a suit, his shoes were polished, and his hair was neatly combed. "How'd you sleep?" I asked.

"Better," he said. "Now let's git goin'."

People at church who knew about the move and his birthday fussed over him, and he was in fine spirits as we headed towards Dale's cabin in Medford. The drive was easy, with good weather and roads. Everyone else was already there, and they all said hello when we arrived, but from my point of view it was an underwhelming welcome. For the first half hour or so, they asked Dad about his new digs and assisted me with his cell phone, but then they returned to normal party activities. It was amazing to me that this move which had been all-consuming for me for several months was just a blip in their lives. They were drinking beer, eating snacks, watching football, chatting, and playing cards as if nothing had really changed. It was then that I realized, for them, this was no big deal. And I wondered how that could be.

Dad enjoyed the afternoon, swapping hunting stories, playing cards, and simply being amid so much family and activity. When I brought out the jams and jelly for distribution, he looked at the label and said to Chris, "We sure are a couple of handsome fellas, huh?" And Chris said, "I hope to hell I look as good as you do when I'm ninety-one!" That was enough of a response for me to feel pleased about my Saturday afternoon efforts. After dinner, we said our goodbyes. Everyone promised that they would come to see Dad at Grace Lodge, but I suspected it would more likely be at the Thanksgiving or

Christmas family gatherings when he saw them again. That was not too far in the future, so it would be OK.

We headed back down the road. A hundred miles later, I pulled up to Grace Lodge in the dark of November. I said to Dad, "Well, did you have a good time?"

"Oh yeah," he assured me. "Thanks for everything. But I'm pretty tired. I think I'll sleep good tonight."

"I hope we both will," I said. "Good night, Daddy."

The Adjustment

Dad gradually settled into life at Grace Lodge. At first, I visited nearly every day. Homer would stop on weekends, but those visits were usual brief pop-ins when we were on our way to somewhere else. Homer and Dad were cordial, but the bond they had once was broken. They never spoke of it, and neither did I. I was grateful that I had moved Dad before an ugly explosion could happen. That would have absolutely broken my heart. It was hard enough the way it was.

As Daddy became accustomed to the Grace Lodge staff and residents, I reduced the frequency of my visits, especially when I was on the road consulting. I always let him know my schedule, when I was leaving and when I was returning, and I called him to check in when I was out of town. He kept to himself in the beginning, mostly reading and watching TV in his room. Maureen and I wanted to see him interact more, and since he had always enjoyed games, I pushed him to join the Bingo group. He resisted at first until he realized there were prizes. He became quite competitive and proudly showed me the quarters he won and stashed away each week. He was especially pleased when I would sit in as the caller, and he would insult me relentlessly if the numbers I announced didn't coincide with his cards. The other residents were taken aback by this banter at first, and a couple of the women scolded him for being so "mean" to me, but they eventually caught on that this was our schtick. Some actually looked forward to it.

The residents were assigned to their tables for meals, and Maureen strategically placed Dad with Bushy Eyebrows, Frank, and Roy. I am sure Bushy Eyebrows had an actual name, but I either never learned it, never remembered it, or both. Bushy never said a lot, but his eyebrows did. He seemed to be in a constant state of amusement generated by the conversation of the other three. Frank was a kidder, and he quickly dubbed my dad "Columbia" because, always cold, Dad wore his winter jacket to every meal, and the brand was emblazoned on the front. I had known Roy from the days of our Adopt a Grandparent program. He had the distinction of being the first Grace Lodge resident, and as a result, the longest. A retired minister, Roy was bright, gentle, kind, and articulate. He was also a dog lover, so he and Daddy often shared dog stories. Dad was the only one at his table who had farmed, so the others asked lots of questions about that. All four men had excellent senses of humor, and there were often explosions of deep laughter coming from their table in an otherwise quiet, genteel atmosphere of mostly women. They were easy-going, capable guys, and the staff enjoyed them as much as they enjoyed each other. Despite that, they did not socialize together outside of meals; perhaps three times a day was plenty.

Grace Lodge also had a cocktail hour with musical entertainment every Thursday, and I encouraged Dad to take part in that. He was reluctant at first, but if he liked the music, he'd attend. I occasionally brought my accordion to play for Dad in his room, and when the staff found out about that, they asked me to play for the other residents, too. Daddy was in his glory on those days. Me, not so much, at least at first, but when I saw how much pleasure it brought the residents, I was happy to do it.

The week of Thanksgiving, Grace Lodge hosted its annual Harvest Dinner. This was a formal affair to which residents were encouraged to invite family and friends. Each table had fall centerpieces and candles. The staff served appetizers and drinks, followed by an extensive buffet dinner. Daddy invited Julie, Jane and me, so for the second time in a month we sat with him and enjoyed a very special meal. He was delighted to have us there. They said to me later that Grace Lodge seemed to agree with him. Had it really only been three weeks since he moved in?

Thanksgiving Day I drove Daddy to Marshfield, and we divided our time between his step-daughter Cindy's celebration, and then Dale's. He was glad to see everyone, and when asked about his new home, he had no complaints. He was especially happy to again be in the company of Ruth's family, and the feeling was clearly mutual. I was reminded of how much change he had been subjected to in the past two years, and it made me sad. His resilience and positivity were beyond impressive, and I was so grateful for that. He could have been angry or apathetic, but instead, he stayed upbeat. I resolved to strive for that same attitude.

On December 8, Maureen met with Daddy and me for his thirty-day review. Maureen had a clipboard and a long list of questions to ask Dad about his life at Grace Lodge. What was going well? What wasn't? How was the food? His room? The facility? His care? His general feeling of well-being and satisfaction? What did he need? What goals would he like to set for himself? When Dad tried to get away with his usual monosyllabic non-answers, Maureen pushed for details. Dad probably spoke more in that hour-long interview than he had ever done in one stretch in his life. It was interesting for me to sit back and just listen for a change. Overall, he seemed pretty happy, but he said that what he missed most of all was playing cards. Nobody at Grace Lodge knew how to play Sheepshead, and that was disappointing. Maureen said, "Well, I'll get on that. I'll bet Brenda, the activities director, can make that happen. So that's my goal—to get you some Sheepshead buddies. But what's yours?"

Dad said he didn't have a goal, didn't need a goal, and thought everything was just fine. Maureen said, "Darlene, what do you think?"

I said, "I think you sit around too much, Dad. When you were at my house, you'd get out and walk. You're not getting enough exercise here, and I'd like to see that change. I think you'd feel better if you got outside, or even walked the halls here."

Maureen agreed with me, and she asked Dad if he might like to set a goal of doing more walking. Dad said, "I walk to the elevator to go to and from meals three times a day. What more do you want?"

Maureen and I looked at each other, and I said, "How about some walks in between?"

When Dad didn't say anything, Maureen suggested, "We'll trade you some card games for some exercise. How's that?" Before he could offer any more resistance, Maureen wrote it on the form, handed her clipboard to Daddy, and said, "Review this, and if you want to add anything, do. If not, sign it and I'll put it in your file so we can look it over again when you have your three-month review. But any time between now and then, if something's on your mind, you let us know, all right? I'll be back to pick up the form before lunch."

As she walked out the door he said, "She runs a tight ship, don't she? We call her "The General." But man, she works hard. She waits on tables, she helps in the kitchen, she runs the programs, she does everything. I better read and sign this paper, because she damn sure will be back for it."

"So, you like her, huh, Dad?"

"Smart, tough woman—just like your ma. Yeah, I like her."

Cards

Maureen was true to her word. Early in December, Brenda walked into Dad's room and said, "I heard you're after a Sheepshead player."

"Yup," Dad said.

"You're lookin' at one," Brenda said. "You know how to play, Darlene?"

"Uh huh," I said.

Brenda nudged Dad and said, "Then let's go."

We followed her to the recreation room, she reached into her pocket for a deck of cards, handed them to my dad and said, "Deal."

For the next hour we played Sheepshead, and as usual, Daddy was on fire. All three of us hurled insults, complained about rotten cards, and laughed, then laughed some more. Dad was happier than he'd been in weeks.

Finally, Brenda said she needed to get going, but that we'd do it again. I said, "Brenda, this is great, but you've got too many responsibilities to be playing cards with my dad and me."

"I'm the activities director," she said, "and this is an activity. If they want to pay me to play cards, let 'em! In the meantime, I'll see if I can drum up some other players. Until then, it's the three of us. And don't think you're going to win all the time, LaVerne. I'll see to that."

"Big talk," Dad said. "Anytime you're ready."

The next week Jenny, who lived next door to Dad, stopped in while we were playing. "Oh, I used to play this game with my late husband!" she exclaimed. "But it's been a long time. I bet I don't remember a thing."

"Pull up a chair," Dad said. "She's a teacher," he said, pointing at me. "She'll help you." It took a while, but slowly the game came back to Jenny, and by the end of the afternoon she had the hang of it. We set a date for early the next week, and then we were four.

The next week Brenda brought along Bob. He had taught with me for years at the high school, and he and his wife had recently moved to Grace Lodge. Bob was suffering from dementia, and although his short-term memory was gone, he still knew how to play his favorite card game. It came as naturally to him as breathing, and he enjoyed the game as much as the rest of us. We played five-handed for a while, and then Brenda excused herself. Four players are enough for a good game of Sheepshead, and despite her earlier claims, Brenda had other things more important than card playing to attend to.

The four of us continued to play cards on a regular basis. We got in the habit of taking turns providing snacks and drinks, and Dad made sure that I kept up our end. No one ever played for money, and no one ever really cared who won or lost. It was enough to shuffle the cards and play. And while Daddy still was not walking as much as he should, at least we'd gotten him out of his room and down the hall on a regular basis. We were all darned happy about that.

More Cards

The wall of residents' mailboxes at Grace Lodge got a lot of attention. Everyone looked forward to mail, a connection to the world they'd for the most part left behind. Too many times I'd seen a resident unlock a mailbox, reach in, and sigh when there was nothing inside. Christmas was coming, and I wanted to be sure that Daddy was not forgotten. One day I said to him, "Daddy, should I pick up some Christmas cards for you to send?"

"No," he answered. "I only send one out when I get one, and I hardly get any, so why bother?"

"Well," I argued, "I send 'em out *so* I get them, that's why. Plus, not many people know that you're here, and they sure don't know your address. So why don't we send some?"

"Too much work," Dad said.

"Look," I countered. "I'll write a letter for you to include with the cards, and all you have to do is sign them, address them, and stamp them. What else have you got to do all day?"

"Oh, all right," he said. "You get the letter written, and we'll go from there. Try to make it sound like me and not some English teacher."

I went home, typed up the letter, and brought it with me the next time I visited. "What do you think?" I said.

"It'll do. But I gotta have addresses and cards and stamps too."

"Gotcha, Chief. I'll get on it. And in the meantime, we have to do something about this room. Doesn't look the least bit like Christmas."

"It's fine," Dad said. "The rest of the damn building is decorated to the nines."

"We'll see," I said.

The next time I stopped, I brought along a little lighted artificial Christmas tree, some cookies and candy, a box of Christmas cards, copies of his letter, an address book, and stamps. "Now this feels more like Christmas," I said. "The rest is up to you."

He did his part. His cards went out, and slowly but steadily, his mailbox yielded responses. Each time I visited, he'd show me his latest haul, most of which also included letters. He kept them on the table near his recliner so that they'd be within easy reach. One day he said, "I think I need some more cards, Kid. I've got a few more people I want to send them to."

"Bet you're glad now that you did this, huh?" I said.

"Well, it's not the dumbest idea you ever had," he acknowledged. "Now, what do you have in mind for my Christmas shopping?"

A Period of Grace

The last few weeks before Christmas were happy ones. I wasn't working much, so I spent more time with Dad. Two of the visits were command performances. The first one was a result of being told that despite staff reminders, Dad wasn't changing his Depends often enough, so it was time for Darlene to step in. Once again, I had to have an awkward hygiene conversation, this time using the arguments that he could easily afford to switch out these adult diapers the minute they were wet, that it was unhealthy not to, and that others were noticing the smell. I pointed out he had boxes of them just sitting in his closet waiting to be used, and he had plenty of time to change them. Did he need help from the staff? "Hell, no!" he exclaimed. "Well, you're going to get it if you don't do it yourself," I assured him. "All right, all right," he muttered, and that was that.

The second command performance was also a hygiene issue. Despite the aides telling Dad that he needed to give up his Columbia parka to be laundered, he steadfastly, albeit politely, refused. Why???? When I asked him what was going on, he said it was clean enough. Obviously not,

I countered, pointing out the food stains and rank odor. "Why don't you just let them launder it?"

"It takes two days," he said.

"Soooooo...why is that a problem?" I asked. "You won't be going outside again until Sunday."

"I need it INSIDE too," he insisted. "You know that I'm cold all the time. I gotta have a coat."

"Well, how 'bout Santa Claus comes early and brings you another winter coat so you can switch back and forth?" I offered.

"That would be OK," he reluctantly agreed, "but it better be a warm one." So off I went to Kohl's, bought him another Columbia parka, and returned to Grace Lodge for an inspection and a fitting. He deemed it acceptable, and before he could even think about putting the old one back on, I grabbed it and handed it over to an aide with the rest of his laundry. Another crisis averted by the mistress of diplomacy...

Most visits were stress free, especially the ones when I brought Daisy and Lily along. He missed having dogs around, and they missed him as well. He kept a stash of Milk Bones in his otherwise empty cupboards, along with a water dish, and biscuits, just in case they got hungry. They'd scamper into his room and up on his lap as soon as they arrived, and they were content to sit with him as he read or watched the birds outside his window. There wasn't a need to make conversation on those days, so I could go through his mail, pay his bills, and balance his checkbook as needed.

We were both looking forward to the family gathering for Christmas at my house. Dad had sent me out with a list and cash for his usual purchase of twenty-some boxes of Zachary chocolates. I asked if he'd like to wrap them himself, and he laughed and said, "Are you kidding? You can do the tags too, as far as I'm concerned."

"Oh no, you don't. You can at least do that, Mister." And he did.

Christmas Eve we attended the candlelight service at church, a lovely prelude to the next day's celebration. Dale and Rosann picked Dad up on their way through town. Rosann couldn't stop talking about how beautiful Grace Lodge was and how lucky Daddy was to have found a place like that. Shortly after they arrived, the rest of the clan descended. We exchanged gifts, ate and drank, played cards, and chatted, just as we had the year before. The women in the family commented privately about how healthy Daddy looked, adding that he must be receiving good care. After a long afternoon of celebrating, everyone got ready to head home, including Dad. That seemed strange and wrong to me, but it was what it was, and there was no turning back. Goodbyes were said, hugs were exchanged, and everyone rushed out the door. It was a blessing, especially for me, that none of us knew that the next time we would all be together would be at Daddy's funeral.

FINAL WINTER

The W(h)iners' Farewell Toast to Daddy, April 2014

Puerta Vallarta

In January of 2014 Homer and I traveled to Puerta Vallarta for a week-long getaway with his cousin Lonna and her husband Jess. We shared their beautiful condo, lounged at the pool and on the beach, reenergizing in the sun. We knew that the dogs were in our friend Sue's capable hands, and that Daddy was also being well-taken care of. It was the first down time for me in a long while, and I needed it. Between the pressures of work and Dad's move, I was exhausted and emotionally spent. It also gave Homer and me an opportunity to spend time together, with no distractions, disagreements, or pressure. There were no visits to Grace Lodge, no phone calls, and no updates on Dad. I felt both liberated and guilty. Had I known what the coming months would bring, perhaps I never would have taken that trip, or maybe I would have stayed in sunny Mexico forever to avoid facing reality.

All things must come to end, so we reluctantly returned home in the coldest part of winter, back to subzero temperatures, endless snow, gray days, and the responsibilities of work and caregiving. It would be a very long time until the coming of spring.

The Real Deal

One of the schools I was working with wanted to recreate an Every Day Heroes project that I had developed with my own students. The idea was for middle schoolers to first create a personal definition of what the word "hero" meant to them. Then they would find people in their lives who fit that definition, interview them about their histories, write essays about what makes them heroic, and finally create related pieces of art. It is helpful to students and teachers to have an example, so I decided to provide one. It's no surprise that I selected Daddy as my hero, and it was fun for me to create both the essay and related video I titled "The Real Deal." The students and staff enjoyed learning about him, and they got to know me better through the project as well. I never said anything to Dad about it, but several months later when I was going through my briefcase, I ran across the essay. As I reread it, I thought, "I bet Daddy would like to have this." So I made a copy, and the next time I visited, I handed it to him when I was about to leave. "This will give you something to read when I'm gone," I said. "I hope you like it."

When I next saw Dad, he didn't mention it. Or the next visit either. Actually, he never did. But not too long after I gave it to him, one of the aides said, "That is such a nice piece that you wrote about your dad."

"Oh, he showed it to you?" I asked.

"Not just to me," she said. "To everybody. All the aides have seen it. And Maureen. And most of the residents. He's got it in the seat of his walker, and he takes it out and has anyone who sits down next to him read it. He's practically worn it out. He's so proud of it."

Really? I thought? *Really????* If she hadn't told me, I never would have known how he felt about it. And to think I almost didn't give it to him. That was typical, though. We just didn't talk about feelings. We never had. I guess we both figured we didn't have to—that we knew how much we appreciated each other. Still, I wished that we said it out loud, at least once in a while. I would have to try to do better, because after a lifetime of unspoken love, it wasn't going to start with him.

The Body Bag

Shortly after our return home from Mexico, I arrived at Grace Lodge for one of my many visits. My heart started pounding when I saw an ambulance parked at the front entrance. Logic told me I would have been called if anything had happened to Dad, but logic was well out of reach at that moment. If not Dad, then who? I knew most of the residents, and I wondered who was suffering, and in what way.

I hurried through the front doors and up the steps to the second floor, preparing myself to see one of the residents being tended to. I was certainly not ready to see two EMTs coming down the hall, carrying a stretcher. And I was even less prepared to see that the stretcher was carrying not a living person, but a body bag. They passed by me in somber silence. I was almost at Dad's room by then, but I was too devastated to walk in and offer a cheery hello. Instead, I went back down the hall to the empty library and tried to slow my breathing and heart rate.

The reality of assisted living centers hit me then as it never had before. It's not assisted living—it's assisted dying. Nobody gets out alive. Anyone who can continue to pay the monthly bills is eventually carried out feet first. While on an intellectual level I had always understood that, this was the first time that the idea truly wrapped itself around my heart. It wasn't my father taking that final journey today, but it would be eventually. I had already watched him decline from someone who could square dance effortlessly to an incontinent old man who needed monthly infusions just to get out of bed and shuffle to his walker every day. What would be next? How could I bear it? How could he? And what other option was there?

    I sat there, cried myself out, dried my tears, washed my face, and then walked back to Daddy's room where he was sitting in his recliner, oblivious to the drama I had just witnessed. I gave him a hug and a kiss, and we sat and chatted just like always, just like nothing had ever happened, and nothing ever would.

The Beginning of the Decline

It had been over two years since I first learned of my father's terminal diagnosis. In all that time, he had held his own. He was still mobile, still eating well, still sound of mind, still quick to laugh. I had grown complacent, thinking that he would live forever. But in late January, all that changed.

It began with his steadily dimming eyesight. He had been near-sighted his whole life, developed and had cataracts removed liked everyone else, but it was glaucoma that was clouding his optimistic view of the world. Despite following his doctor's rigid regimen of regular appointments and daily eyedrops, the disease steadily progressed. I had replaced the standard library books I borrowed to only those with large print, but I noticed Daddy wasn't reading much at all anymore. One Sunday when he closed the cover on one, he said, "That's it. No more books."

"Didn't you like it?" I asked.

"I can't see to read," he replied. "I guess I'm done with that now too. At least I can still watch TV." I had no idea that his vision had declined that much. Like everything else, he didn't announce it, give play-by-plays, or complain. He just accepted it and moved on.

It seems to me now that I discovered on Sundays much of what was happening with his health. One morning I arrived to pick him up for church, and he was dressed and sitting in his chair, anticipating my arrival. "Ready?" I asked.

"I guess," he said.

"You don't sound too sure," I joked.

"Well, I'm a little confused," he admitted.

"Didn't you sleep well?" I probed.

"I can't remember," he said. "I don't remember going to bed. I woke up on the john."

"What??? Are you saying you spent the whole night on the toilet?" I demanded.

"I guess so," he said. "When I finally came to, it was time to get ready for church."

"Holy smokes," I said. "We'd better skip church and talk to somebody about this."

"Why?" he countered. "I'm fine, I'm up and dressed, so let's go to church. I can eat when we get back." He was clearly done discussing it, so off we went, but it's all I thought about during church and for days after.

A few weeks later, Maureen stopped me in the hall. "How's your dad doing?" she asked.

"OK, I think," I said, "why do you ask?"

"Maybe it's nothing," she said, "He didn't come down for breakfast until 9:30 yesterday, and he's *always* at the table by 7. When I reminded him breakfast ends at 9, he seemed confused. I don't think he had any idea what time it was. He laughed it off, but it's concerning. I thought you should know."

Yes, it was indeed concerning. And there was more to come. Shortly after that incident, Maureen reported that Daddy hadn't come down for breakfast at all one morning.

When one of the aides went to check on him, he was still in bed. "Get up, Sleepyhead," she said.

"I can't," he answered with a grin.

"Why not?" she persisted.

"Legs won't let me," he said simply. "So, I'm just layin' here until they do." She called for help, and in due course, he was up and walking with his walker as if nothing had ever happened. No one was able to explain it, and he was back to being mobile, so we moved on, but it was clear that things were changing, and not in a good way.

In the following weeks, he navigated across the snow-covered church parking lot with his walker each Sunday, but he insisted on using his cane to get to the altar for Communion. Even though I was right beside him, I always breathed easier when we returned to our seats. The pastor recognized what was happening and offered to serve Daddy Communion in the pew as he did several other elderly members. Daddy acquiesced, and he didn't complain, but I know it embarrassed him to have to remain seated.

One Sunday I noticed he wasn't opening his hymnal anymore and joining in the singing. He loved music, so I knew something was very wrong. I snuck a look at him during the sending hymn and watched tears slowly coursing down his old cheeks. When we got back into the car, I asked why he hadn't been singing. "Can't read the words," he said, "Can't read the bulletin. Can't take Communion. No point in going to church like this. I'm done with it. You'll just have to go for both of us." I could see that he had made up his mind, so there was no point in arguing. But that didn't stop my heart from breaking. Church had been so important to him for so long. What next?

That question was answered a few Sundays later. I walked into Grace Lodge to a flurry of activity in the dining room. Daddy was the center of attention. He was lying on the floor, with several aides assessing the situation. "Dad!" I exclaimed. "What the heck happened???"

He looked up at me benignly and grinned. "I guess I got tired and just laid down."

"This isn't funny," I said.

"No, it isn't," one of the aides said. "We want to call an ambulance, but he says no. Maybe he'll let you take him to the hospital to be checked out."

"Nope," Dad said. "Ain't nothin' broken. I can tell. Stop all the fuss and help me up."

We got him to his feet, seated him at the table, and he ate lunch as if nothing had ever happened. There was no way he was going to let me drive him to the hospital, and that was that.

As the days and weeks passed, I never knew what to expect when I arrived. Most visits were uneventful, with regular conversation, banter, and card playing. But I got to where I dreaded seeing the approach of Maureen because she usually had more bad news to share. The latest development was that Dad had developed a strange mannerism of rubbing his teeth at lunch. Maureen said it seemed involuntary and when she pointed it out to him, he said, "I do??" Another time when I visited, she reported that Dad had not come down for lunch at all. This was unusual behavior, and when they checked, he seemed to have again lost track of time.

"Have you ever heard of a TIA?" Maureen asked me. "It stands for transient ischemic attack. People often call it a mini stroke. It's short term—can last just a few minutes or a few hours, and often it doesn't seem to cause any permanent damage. I think that's what's happening with your dad. It's not life-threatening, but it's a sign of things to come. Be sure to let his doctor know what's going on and watch for other erratic behaviors. This is likely to get worse." I had heard about the same thing happening to my friends' parents, and although this wasn't news to me, I was heartsick. It seemed that Daddy and I were the only two passengers on a speeding train that had already left the station.

Near the end of March, I was scheduled to attend and present at a three-day conference in Milwaukee. I had misgivings about leaving town, but Maureen assured me that Dad was in good hands and that a change in focus would probably be good for me. The conference went well, and it seemed that she had been right, until I stopped in to see my dad on my way home. Daddy was lying on the floor when I walked into his room. Maureen was kneeling beside him, asking the standard stroke questions, and when she asked him if he knew her name, he stared at her ID and read, "Maureen. It says it right there." Then he laughed. Although it was clear to everyone else that this was no laughing matter, Dad went right for the joke. Maureen called the nurse, who continued the questions and checked his vital signs. He was confused, his speech was slurred, and his face was slack on one side. Maureen told me that when he had been sitting in the dining room earlier at lunch, he didn't seem to remember that he had an apartment at Grace Lodge. When we had him safely tucked in bed, Maureen said to both of us, "This is getting serious now. I'm sure neither of you wants to hear this, but it's time to involve hospice. Do you want me to help you get that started?"

Before Dad could protest, I said, "Yes, please. You know the ropes. We don't. We're going to need some help here, Daddy. Is that all right?"

"You worry too much," Daddy mumbled. "But if it makes you feel better, it's OK with me."

It didn't make me feel better at all. But what else was there to do?

Hospice

The hospice team arrived April 1, and the significance of the date was not lost on me. We met nurses, social workers, and volunteers. We filled out reams of paperwork, and Daddy sat in his recliner and watched as a crew moved in a hospital bed. And a wheelchair. And a commode. No more walker. No more independent showers or trips to the bathroom. Homer helped me move the twin bed and desk we had borrowed back to Tracey's house. Daddy's cozy little apartment was looking less and less like a home and more and more like a hospital room. Thankfully, the stroke didn't seem to leave any long-term effects. Daddy's speech and face had returned to normal, and his thinking was clear. In his typical fashion, he talked about the details of his days but not about what loomed ahead. Apparently, he felt it wasn't worthy of discussion, and I didn't know how to approach it either. As always, we avoided talking about feelings; they were simply understood. Still, I wanted to spell it out. At the end of one visit, I left him a card that said, "I can't understand this journey or take it for you, but I will be beside you every step of the way. All my love, Darlene."

The next time I stopped in, I greeted him, as I always did, with "How you doin', Daddy?"

He looked at me, and said simply, "I'm dyin', Kid. That's how I'm doin'."

I sat down next to him and said, "Are you scared?"

"Nope," he said. "Had to happen eventually. Nobody lives forever. In the meantime, the bird feeder needs to be filled. Get on it, would ya?" End of that Hallmark moment.

Before Christmas, I had made plans to visit Sarah in Florida in April. The flight was paid for, and she was expecting me. Now I had serious misgivings about making the trip, but when I spoke to the hospice nurse about Dad's prognosis, she said he could have weeks to months to live, and there was no reason to cancel. I talked to Daddy about it too, and he said, as always, that I worry too much, that he would be just fine, that they were taking good care of him, that I could use a break. So, with great reluctance, I drove to Madison, dropped my car at Ken's, and took an early morning bus to O'Hare to catch my flight. The weather had other ideas. The flight was delayed once. Then again. Then yet again. I spent the entire day in the airport, watching the monitors for updates as the hands of the clock slowly marked each passing hour. I wondered if this weren't some sort of cosmic sign that I shouldn't be making this trip at all. The flight was delayed yet again. The airline representative said it might or might not leave at all that evening; there was no way of knowing. I had the option to cancel the ticket. I checked the bus schedule and saw that the last bus back to Madison was due to leave in an hour. If I didn't catch it and the flight was delayed again, I would have to spend the night in the airport, and who knew if or when we would get out the next day. "The hell with it," I decided. "I think God is talking to me." I called Sarah, Ken, and Homer to announce my change in plans and grabbed the last bus heading north. I spent the night at Ken's and drove back home in the morning.

"Short trip," Dad said when I strolled into his room. I

filled him in on what had happened, and he asked if the flight ever left for Florida.

"Yup," I said. "Turns out it took off about the same time I was getting on the bus."

"Shoulda figured that," he said. But I could tell he was glad to see me, and I knew that I was glad to see him.

I have never regretted missing that flight. Each time I saw him, Daddy continued to decline by degrees, sometimes subtle, others drastic. One morning as I was headed to his room, his favorite aide Jane stopped to talk. She spent a lot of time with him, and because she was always whistling when she came into his room, he affectionately called her Shitbird, just like the red-winged blackbirds who frequented his feeder. Red-winged blackbirds had been almost as ubiquitous as manure on Dad's farm, and although we never regarded them as the nuisance that sparrows and grackles were, they were certainly not special. However, since we had none around our house in Rhinelander, he enjoyed seeing them again when he moved to Grace Lodge. While "Shitbird" would probably be viewed as an insult coming from anyone else, Jane recognized this moniker as the high compliment Dad intended. I liked Jane very much, and I knew that she had a very good relationship with my father.

"How's he doing?" I asked.

"He's OK," she said, "but he's worried about you."

"Me???? I asked. "Why is he worried about *me*?"

"He says you're taking this hard," Jane answered. "He's worried about how you're going to cope when he goes."

"He told you that? He never tells me anything about how he feels."

"He doesn't know how to," Jane said gently. "And he doesn't think he has to. He figures you know, that you've always known. He loves you so much. I hope it's OK that I said something." I was so grateful that she had, that she was so good to him, and that he had someone that he could be honest with, even if it wasn't me.

    I dried my tears and headed into Dad's room. We had arranged for an impromptu Sheepshead game since I wasn't in Florida, and I wheeled him to the rec room. Bob, Jenny, Dad, and I played for an hour or so, with Brenda stopping in to check on our progress. Dad was playing well, and he was merciless about proclaiming his prowess. The laughter was loud and long, and winner and losers alike had a wonderful time. That was the last card game we would ever have, and looking back, it was better than any trip to Florida. God knew what He was doing when He delayed that flight.

Dwindling

As the days passed, Dad ate less and less, becoming increasingly weak. Even trips to the nearby commode were exhausting. He reluctantly acquiesced when the hospice nurse urged a catheter, and although she said he didn't so much as flinch when it was inserted, I knew that the whole ordeal was humiliating for him, especially the presence of the urine collection bag. When I mentioned it to Julie, she immediately designed and sewed discreet fabric covers that she dropped off the next day. It was no big deal to her, but it was a kindness that pleased Dad immensely and that I will never forget. My friends were so steadfast and wonderful. I don't know what I would have done without them.

By this time Daddy was eating only breakfast; his appetite had dwindled to almost nothing. I brought in Boost and milkshakes, and for about a week, he seemed to enjoy those, but soon he lost interest in them as well. He had always been thin, and he was steadily losing weight. Since he couldn't bathe or shave himself, the aides were a regular fixture in his room. I got to know them all well, and I was so grateful for them. Because he was so weak, he spent almost all his time bedridden. Despite regular repositioning, he began to develop bedsores. Sarah had watched the same thing happen to her mom, so she sent me a homeopathic recipe the moment I mentioned it. It may not have done much good, but at least I felt I was doing something.

Nancy

Ironically and predictably, as Dad became more and more ill, he attracted a steady stream of visitors. My cousin Nancy was the first. They had always had a special affection for each other. When I told her what was happening, she dropped everything to drive over from the Twin Cities. I knew he would be very pleased and surprised to see her. When we walked into his room, I said happily, "Look who's here, Dad!" She leaned over to give him a hug, something I rarely did. He opened his eyes, reached for his glasses, and I said, "So how'd you sleep, Dad?"

"OK," he muttered without taking his eyes off her. Not to be ignored, I continued, "Did you have any good dreams?"

"What the hell kind of stupid question is that??" he exploded. "I slept. Just like always. I don't dream. And I'm sick of your goddamn questions!!!" The subsequent extended silence was deafening.

That's the first and last time I can ever remember Dad yelling at me. I was absolutely crushed, and I could not imagine where that level of hostility had come from. My eyes filled with tears, and I turned away and looked out the window so that he wouldn't see. Nancy's face indicated she too was shocked by his outburst and fully sympathetic.

She immediately turned to him, smoothed his blankets with kind hands, and eased the tension with loving small talk. Eventually, I pulled myself together. Dad acted as if nothing had ever happened. But I will never forget it. I wonder now how much other unspoken anger he had tamped down, and what I might have done to avoid it festering or developing in the first place. I worried that this kind of aggression was going to replace his good-natured personality that I had always enjoyed. Despite my hurt and fears, that was his first and last outburst. I still don't know what prompted it, but I do know that he was more than entitled to it. I can't imagine anyone who could have shown more grace or dignity while dying.

Nancy commented on the beautiful view outside Dad's window and observed that because of the poor placement of his hospital bed, he couldn't enjoy it or the birds at his feeder. She immediately came up with a better furniture arrangement, and it wasn't long after that Dad was gazing out his window at the snow-covered river and trees. It was a much better view than the stark wall he had been facing. They chatted a bit more, and before long Daddy fell silent, then absently began rubbing his teeth, back and forth, back and forth, back and forth. Nancy looked at me questioningly, and I shrugged. Eventually he fell asleep.

As a nurse who had witnessed her own parents' decline, Nancy knew that this was probably the last visit she would ever have with Dad. We spent most our time at his bedside, chatting with him or each other when he slept. The next morning, she hugged and kissed him, and then me, goodbye. It had been wonderful to see her again, to feel her love and support. She assured me that she would be in touch.

A few days later, I was sitting with my dad, and we could clearly hear the geese on the river singing a love song to us, a sure sign of renewal and spring. The next day I received an email from Lonna, whom we had joined in Mexico in January. She had written:

"Hi to all my art teachers and friends. I must admit that I was disappointed after my flat sales at a recent exhibit so now I need to share my good news. The City of Peoria is purchasing one of my pieces for its permanent collection. I entered their last art show, Celebration of Art, a few weeks ago. I do not even know if I won anything as I have not yet had time to even go over there to see the exhibit. The piece is a large clayboard with black India ink entitled "Wild Geese." I was deeply and forever moved by Mary Oliver's great poem, "Wild Geese." I could hear the wild geese calling my name as I worked on this piece after a particular time of intense grief. Hope my success encourages you as it did me." Attached was a photo of her magnificent piece of art and the poem. Thirteen words leapt out at me. "...Meanwhile the world goes on...Meanwhile the wild geese...are heading home again..."

The timing of all of this was uncanny and so comforting. When I shared it with Nancy, she wrote, "I watched a lone goose across the river from Grace Lodge on Monday and Tuesday... Remembering that, seeing this and reading this, I am moved to tears. And I do not understand why a Man of the Earth should need to leave it in the Springtime, of all times, unless it is intended that the rebirth of spring is meant to soothe and begin the healing of the hearts of those left behind."

Glad All Over

As winter dragged on and on, the snow remained piled high outside Dad's window, and the icicles hung down ever longer. It seemed that winter would never leave. I wanted to somehow brighten up Dad's room, and I knew exactly what he needed. I just was not quite sure that I could make it happen.

I grabbed my coat and headed to my favorite florists. They already knew of the long gladiola history between my dad and me, and I was sure that if anyone could find these late summer favorites in the dead of winter, it would be them.

"We don't have any in stock," they apologized when I explained what I wanted. "Wrong season. We might be able to order them, but they'll be expensive. Would you like to try something else?"

"No, it has to be glads," I specified.

"I'll contact our distributors and see what we can do," the owner said. "But I won't know until tomorrow, and even if they have them, it will take a couple of days. Is that OK?"

"It has to be," I said. "I don't know how much time Daddy has, but this will mean a lot to him. And me too. Just call me and let me know, OK?"

"Will do," she said. The next day she called to report

that she had found glads, but that they were going to be costly. Did I still want the arrangement?

"Absolutely," I assured her. "And please put a rush on it."

I was there two days later when the flowers arrived. The glads, while not summer quality and certainly inferior to anything my father would have grown, stood tall and proud in the vase I set beside his bed.

"What do you think, Daddy?" I asked.

"They're nice," he said. "Funny to see 'em this time of year. Where'd you get them?"

"None of your beeswax," I said. "Just enjoy."

To be honest, they didn't hold up very long or very well. I think now that they had very little to do with Daddy, and everything to do with my attempting to deny the reality of winter and death. I was trying to preserve a tradition that was out of season, foolish, but thus perhaps all the more precious. I don't remember what those flowers actually cost, but it was a lot. I remember thinking Daddy could have planted an entire garden of bulbs for the same amount, and he would have been appalled by the bill. I didn't care. I still don't. I wrote the check and dropped it off at the florist, thanking her profusely for going the extra mile. I am still glad I bought him those flowers, and that they were there when he was still well enough to look at them and remember sunny summer days.

Affirmation

There was heavy snow in the forecast, and I wasn't sure if the roads would be open enough for me to drive in the next day, so I decided to spend most of April 15 with Dad. It was a sweet rare, good day, despite the coming storm. Dad was a little more confused than normal when I arrived that morning, and it concerned me. The social worker Linda recognized that too when she saw him. She said, "Good morning, LaVerne. How are you doing?"

"Good," he said. "My daughter is here."

"Is she a pretty good daughter?" Linda asked.

My heart sank as I anticipated his answer, and I found myself holding my breath. Who knew what he might say? On a good day, my father was more likely to make a smart-ass remark than a sincere answer, and in his confused state, there was no way of predicting what he might say. I only knew that I would remember whatever he said for the rest of my life, and I prayed it would be positive. The seconds ticked by slowly, and it seemed that Daddy had forgotten the question, when he finally looked at me and said, "She's...great." That moment still is one of the happiest of my life.

Later that day the chaplain came to visit. I excused myself and got up to leave when she offered him communion, but she urged me to stay and join them. I sat back down, and as she led us through this familiar rite of sharing the Eucharist, Daddy seemed at peace. She asked him if there were anything in particular he wished to pray for, and he said, "No, but thank you, God, for a good, long life. And thank you for my family." His voice was strong and steady as he repeated the Lord's Prayer, confidently finishing, "for thine is the kingdom, and the power, and the glory, forever and ever. Amen."

"Amen," I repeated with a long sigh, and it was then I realized I had been again holding my breath. Not just during the prayer, but for the last several weeks. My friends and I have a motto that we share to get through tough times: "One step. One breath." It reminds us to be mindful of the now, to not look too far ahead, to not try to manage the uncertain future, only the present moment. Daddy had clearly been doing a far better job than I had of exemplifying that mantra, and his quiet, firm faith reminded me that his future was not in my hands. I found peace in that as I again drove away from Grace Lodge that dark winter evening.

More Company

A few days later Nancy's brother Gordie and his girlfriend Marla came over for a visit. Dad seemed to recognize him, but it was hard to tell for sure. As was typical for them, despite their best efforts, Gordie and Marla bickered over things of little or no consequence, and I think Dad was relieved to see them go. After they left, he turned to me and said, "Who was that guy?"

"That was Nancy's brother Gordie—your nephew. Uncle Dick's son? Remember? He came over from Minnesota to see you."

"He did?" Dad asked. "I don't know who he was or who that woman he was with either, but they sure didn't seem to connect, did they?" Even in his confusion, he got that right. Then he closed his eyes and began rubbing his teeth, again, again, again.

As Easter approached, more and more company arrived. Ken was the next to visit. He and Daddy had never been close, and Ken was pressed for time, so it was a short stay, but I know Dad appreciated his making the trip, and Ken would be returning the next week.

Uncle Neal was in no condition to travel from Kansas to visit Daddy, but Nancy had called and apprised him of Dad's failing health. One afternoon the phone rang, and it was Neal, asking to speak to Dad. Daddy was tickled to hear from him, and they reminisced for a few minutes about their long-ago youth. Neal said he was sorry he couldn't come see him, and that he was going to miss him. They were straightforward and honest in their goodbyes, and it pleased them both to say their farewells, even if it was across a thousand miles of phone lines. Neal asked Dad to hand the phone to me again, and when he did, my uncle said, "Would you get some flowers for your dad for me? I want him to have them now, while he's still alive to enjoy them, not at the funeral. Just let me know what they cost, and I'll send you the money."

"Will do," I said. "I'll get right on it."

The next day I walked in with an aromatic bouquet of Stargazer lilies, another flower Daddy had loved growing. "From Uncle Neal," I said. "Aren't they pretty?"

"That Neal," Daddy said, "Prince of a guy." It wasn't the first time he'd ever said that, but it would be the last.

I called Neal and told him that the flowers had arrived, that Daddy was delighted with them, that I had taken pictures and would send him a photo in the mail. Neal wanted to know what they had cost, and I said that I didn't have the bill yet, but I would include it in the letter with the picture.

I sent the photo to Uncle Neal with a card of thanks, but despite repeated pressure from him, I never told him the cost or let him pay for that bouquet. It was enough that he had thought of doing it, and that he called to make it happen. Although he couldn't be there in person, his visit was perhaps the most significant of them all.

On Good Friday, there was a boatload of company—the hospice aide, my friend Terri, Heidi from church, Dad's grandson Chris and family. Daddy was in a good mood, full of smart aleck remarks until we wore him out. Then it was back to silence and teeth rubbing. He wasn't getting any better, but he wasn't much worse than earlier in the week. He was still pain-free and cognizant of the world around him. The next day would be the first family gathering without him, since it was in Marshfield, and he was in no condition to travel. Homer and I drove south alone, and there was nothing joyous about the event as far as I was concerned. The rest of the family seemed oblivious to Dad's situation. There was exactly one question about how Dad was doing, and none about me. I should have known better than to expect anything more, but it hurt just the same. I silently thanked God for the family of friends I had self-selected. Once again, I was reminded of their sustaining role in my life.

Easter

Dale and Roseann drove north to visit Daddy for a few hours Easter Sunday. He was happy to see them, well enough to have a chat, and gracious enough to share his stash of jelly beans, even the coveted black ones. But he was pretty out of it by the time they left. Hospice called the next day to tell me that Daddy was running a fever of 100.5. They were giving him Tylenol to try to bring it down. When I got there, he had removed his hospital gown and was sprawled across the bed, naked except for his briefs, practically falling out of bed. This, the man who was always cold. He was also agitated, almost manic, but very funny and getting along great with the aides. They got him into the gown again, straightened him out and repositioned the bedding, then gave him more Tylenol and Lorazepam, the latter an anti-anxiety med. I played my accordion for him, and he was out like a light within forty minutes and pretty much stayed that way until I left around 3. The hospice nurse said the Lorazepam would help ensure that he didn't try to get out of bed. She added that the fever might be a blip on the radar or the beginning of the end—there was just no way of knowing. I prayed for a speedy, gentle ending and resurrection. What more was there to do?

Monday and Tuesday

Throughout this flurry of visitors, Homer remained hospitable but at the same time detached. He thought that people were blowing things out of proportion, and that Dad would be around for considerably more time. He rarely visited him when I went, but he listened to my daily report. I knew Homer's mind was more on the upcoming National Rifle Association convention in Indiana than on Dad. He said he wanted to go to the convention which would be held April 25-27, but he'd stay home if I preferred. He'd be gone most of a week, but he assured me that Dad would still be alive when he returned. I knew better, but I insisted he go. To be honest, it was a relief to know he would be gone. Daddy and I had traveled most of this road without him, and it seemed that it should be just the two of us at the end. I didn't think I could deal with Homer's seeming indifference on top of the grief of saying goodbye to my father. By this time, I was spending almost all day every day at Grace Lodge, so it wasn't like I would be home much anyway.

Monday while I was visiting Dad, Linda walked in. Besides being the hospice social worker, she had also been my next-door neighbor for many years. We had never been close, but we had shared history and proximity to connect us, and she was very good at her job. She checked in with Dad, made some small talk, and then beckoned me into the hallway.

"How's he doing?" I asked.

"That's what I wanted to talk to you about," she said. "He says he thinks he's getting better."

"He *what??*" I exclaimed. "You can't be serious. He's not, is he???"

"No, he's not," Linda said gently.

"How much time does he have?" I probed.

"Impossible to say, Darlene," she said. "There is just no way to know. We've had this talk before."

"I know," I admitted. "I know it's crazy to want a timetable for death, but if I only had some idea what to expect. This is just so damned hard."

"It's harder for him," she reminded me. "Have you given him permission to go?"

"What do you mean?" I asked.

"Sometimes patients just need to be told that you accept that they can't stay. Your dad is worried about how you will cope with his passing. Rather than think about that, he's pretending that this isn't really happening."

"But that's crazy," I said, "I don't want him to die, of course, but I'll be OK."

"I know that, and you know that, but he doesn't," Linda said. "I think you should tell him." Then she gave me a hug and headed down the hall.

I took a deep breath and walked back into Dad's room. I sat down on the edge of his bed and waited until he opened his eyes. Then I said, "Daddy, did you ever think we would end up together like this?

"Nope," he said.

"Well, I did," I said. "I knew all along that one day we would be here. I've been blessed to have had you all these years, especially these last two. I love you so much. But

I know that you're tired, and you're hurting, and you're not having any fun. Mom and Ruth are waiting for you, and when you're ready, you just go. I'll miss you like crazy, but I'll be OK. You raised me to be tough and strong, you know."

"Sure did," he said. "Sure as hell did." And then he squeezed my hand, grinned, and drifted off to sleep.

When I arrived at Grace Lodge the next morning, Dad's situation was grim: shallow breathing, rapid heartbeat, loss of appetite, sad, sunken eyes, pallor, reduction in interaction and banter with the staff. He still managed to respond to "How you doin'?" with a whispered "Still kickin'" and an attempt at a grin.

The hospice chaplain came in for communion. Dad managed a sliver of wafer that he never did swallow, but he joined us in the Lord's Prayer. I offered a prayer of thanksgiving for the wonderful man, father, husband, grandfather, and great grandfather he was, and requested a gentle departure. I was satisfied as I left for home that I had said everything I needed to say.

On Tuesday after Homer had left, I loaded Lily and Daisy into the car and headed into town. I thought their visit would cheer my dad up, and I knew they were missing spending time with me. But the canine visit did not go well. They were restless, and when I tried to put them in bed with Dad, they growled and fought with each other and clamored all over him until he asked me to take them away. It made me sad that the same dogs who once brought him so much companionship and comfort were now such an unpleasant intrusion. I needed to take them home, but they had a vet appointment, and I was reluctant to leave Dad's bedside. I called Terri to ask for help.

When I explained my problem, she said, "We've got this. Is your house open? George can take them to the vet and then home. I'm off this afternoon and will be up to keep you company. Hang in there. And don't tell me you can't ask us to do that. I volunteered."

Once again, as I hung up the phone, I thanked God for the blessing of my friends.

Another Step, Another Breath

I think it was mid-week by then. It would be dishonest to say that I am absolutely certain of the chronology of everything I have written here. The last weeks of my father's life seem to be indelibly, albeit foggily, etched in my memory. There are key moments that are absolutely clear to me, but the context is often cloudy. Perhaps that doesn't matter. The story, after all, truly belongs to him and me, and I am the only one left to tell it.

Daddy was steadily failing, and it had to be apparent to anyone who knew him. One afternoon Brenda came in and asked him if he wanted to play a few hands of cards. "No, I don't think so," he said. "I just don't feel up to it anymore." Brenda and I both knew that was a very bad sign. Although the hospice team still refused to make predictions about how much time he had left, it was no coincidence that they were checking on him more frequently.

I called Dad's favorite singer, my friend Sue, who often took care of the dogs for us when needed, and asked if she would do me the favor yet again if I wanted to stay at Grace Lodge. I was becoming more and more afraid of receiving an emergency phone call in the night and of being unable to arrive in time given the distance and winter roads. She assured me that she would take care of everything and do what I needed. I packed a few toiletries and a spare set of clothes so I would be ready. All I had to do was tell her when, and she would be there.

The next morning, I left the house with my overnight bag, a book, my crocheting, and my phone in hand. I wanted to have something to occupy my time in the hours that loomed ahead. One look at Dad when I arrived assured me that I had been wise to plan for a long day. He was having trouble taking in fluids, and when Linda came, she showed me how to swab his mouth with a wet sponge to make him more comfortable. He was less responsive than he had been, and I was worried.

Linda chatted with him a bit, but he said little or nothing more. I followed her into the hall, and she said, "I don't think he has a whole lot more time, Darlene. You should probably let your family know."

"How much time?" I probed.

"As I've said before," Linda answered, "we can't be sure. But I would guess just a few days. Make the most of them."

"Should I plan to stay here?" I asked.

"That's up to you," Linda replied. "You need to take care of yourself, too. The drugs we're giving him are keeping him comfortable, and there's nothing you can really do for him."

"Except be there for him," I said. "Make sure that he doesn't die alone like Mom did. I'm going to stay."

"You can only do that for so long," Linda advised. "Call on family and friends to relieve you from time to time."

"My brother is coming Saturday," I assured her. "I can handle this until then. In the meantime, I've got friends to lean on."

"Feel free to call any time if you need us," Linda said. "Hospice is available 24-7. This is what we're all about."

I thanked her, and she gave me a warm hug before she

headed out the door. Daddy was rubbing his teeth again, a habit to which I was beginning to become accustomed. It seemed to soothe him somehow, and often it led to his falling back asleep. It did once again.

I went out into the hall to call Ken and Sue. Ken said he was still planning to arrive Saturday morning, and Sue assured me that she would take care of the dogs until further notice. I also emailed the W(h)iners with an update and said that under the circumstances I wouldn't be joining them for drinks the next evening. Then I returned to Dad's room and his comfortable lift chair. I had no way of knowing when I bought it the previous summer that I would be spending so many hours in it keeping vigil.

I reached for the afghan I was working on and began to crochet. The pattern was familiar, the stitches easy, the effort methodical and mindless, which is just what I needed. I worked for several hours until I discovered the flaw I had been repeating, row after row. "Damn," I muttered. "Did it again." I began tearing out the afghan, winding the yards and yards of yarn into an-ever growing ball. This was not a new experience for me. Dad used to joke that I got more mileage out of yarn than any woman he knew because I ripped it out and reused it so much. "Good thing you don't just throw it away," he'd say. "You couldn't afford this stupid hobby if you did." As I ripped and wrapped, ripped and wrapped, I felt Dad's eyes on me. I looked up and found him staring at my disappearing progress. He didn't say anything for a long time, just watched me in silence. Finally, he shook his head in disgust, watched me for a few more seconds, and then muttered, "You're a goddamn fool."

I burst out laughing. This time he hadn't hurt my feelings at all. He was so incredibly right. How many times had I done this? Too many to count, and I knew there would be many more in the future. "I sure am, Daddy," I admitted. "You'd think I would know better than this by now, wouldn't you? But I obviously don't. I'm a fool, all right—but I'm your fool, and you're stuck with me." He returned to rubbing his teeth, I returned to tearing out row after row, and once more he fell asleep.

Later that afternoon he woke again. "Hey," I greeted him. "How are you doing?"

"OK," he said. "When did you get here?"

"Oh, I've been here a while," I said. "Just sittin' here watchin' you sleep. Your girlfriends have been in and out checking up on you. Do you need anything?"

"Mouth is dry," he muttered. "Always dry."

I sponged his mouth out again as best I could, realizing how awkward and ill at ease I was. Having never had children or been anyone else's caregiver, I was a terrible nurse. I didn't have a clue about how to feed, bathe, shave, change diapers, lift, turn, medicate—any of the host of tasks my father's comfort depended on. It was laughable to think that I had once considered nursing as a career. It was even more ridiculous that I had imagined I could manage his care by myself, in my home in the middle of nowhere, without the help of an experienced 'round the clock staff. For the first time since moving Dad into Grace Lodge, I realized the wisdom of this decision. I summoned one of the aides who was there in a jiffy to attend to Dad's needs as I said a silent prayer of thanks.

Once we were again alone, Daddy returned to rubbing his teeth. I sat in silence and watched him. It was interesting to me that he had told the staff a few weeks prior that he didn't want to brush his teeth anymore, and just as interesting that they told him he had to. "What's the point?" he said. "I'm not gonna need 'em much longer."

"Well, you need them now," one said, "and anyway, what else do you have to do?" So, the twice a day dental ritual continued, joined now by this fixation. Dad must have become conscious of my staring at his moving fingers, slowed the rubbing, then stopped completely. He looked at me and announced, "I'm about done farting around here." Then his hand, which had stilled for a minute, returned to the incessant motion. Somehow, I knew that Dad had just announced to me his intention to die, in his characteristic, understated, colloquial farmer's way. He was about done farting around with ninety-one years of living; what else was there to say?

When Maureen stopped in his room, I told her that I planned to spend the night with Dad, if that was that OK. She asked me if I was sure I wanted to do that and cautioned me that this might be the first of many sleepless nights ahead. I said I knew that, but I wanted to stay anyway. She then suggested I might be more comfortable sleeping in a vacant room down the hall. I thanked her for the generous offer but said I'd be fine in Dad's recliner snuggled under a blanket. I wanted to be able to hear his breathing. She reminded me that since it was Thursday, the residents would gather for cocktails at 4, and I was welcome to join them. A glass of wine would do me good, she said. Then she gave Daddy's hand a squeeze and went on her way.

One glass of wine? I smiled as I thought an entire box might serve me better. It certainly couldn't impair my crocheting any more than being sober had. I settled back in Dad's recliner and picked up my yarn and hook to try again. At about 4:30, there was a knock on the door. There stood Maureen's handsome young son who sometimes volunteered at the Thursday social hours. He had a tumbler of chardonnay in one hand and a glass of ice in the other. "My mom said to deliver this to you," he shyly explained. "She said she was pretty sure you needed it." He set the glasses down on the table next to me, then added, "She said to tell you there's more where that came from, but you might want to come down for supper to go with it." Then he quietly took his leave.

Such a lovely, caring gesture, I thought. She didn't have to do that. And it wasn't just because it was my dad and me. She went the extra mile for all the residents. I was so grateful for her presence.

I added the ice to the wine and sipped it as I read my email. Beth had sent a message on behalf of all the W(h)iners, asking if it would be all right for them to convene at Grace Lodge the next day rather than our local watering hole. They wanted to be with me to offer their support. She assured me that they didn't want to intrude, but if I wanted them there, they would come armed with glasses, wine, and a corkscrew. I thought it was a wonderful idea, and emailed an enthusiastic "Yes, please!" to their offer.

I sat next to Dad's bed the rest of Thursday evening, reading and crocheting and watching quietly as the night shift aides came and went. When the lights went out, I listened to his irregular breathing and tried to quiet my mind until I was finally able to fall asleep. I woke a dozen times throughout the night, held my breath until I heard Daddy's, looked at the clock, and willed morning to bring the gift of one more day.

The W(h)iners' Farewell

Friday finally dawned, but I remember nothing about the morning or most of the afternoon. Daddy was becoming less and less responsive, and he spoke very little. I told him that the W(h)iners were coming to see him after school, and that he should get ready for some noise. I also told him to be prepared to be surrounded by seven drinking women who knew and loved him. He seemed to understand, but he didn't comment. I wondered how this would go, but I knew we would move our gathering down the hall if it was too much for Dad to deal with.

Around 4, my women, my rocks, the sisters who kept me upright, arrived one by one. I introduced them to Daddy, reminding him of their names, and each spoke to him, squeezed his hand, stroked his arm, or gave him a hug. They quietly moved down to the rec room which I had reserved for our assembly while I waited for the next friend to appear. When all had gathered, I told Dad that I would be back shortly. The long bingo table in the rec room was covered with wine glasses and bottles, and the chatter and laughter of my steadfast friends of over thirty years filled the room. They surrounded me with their love and arms, poured wine and solace, and then settled down to ask how it was going. I told them it had been a very long week, but it was better now. We caught up for a bit, and then Julie said, "I think we need to go raise a glass to LaVerne. What do you think, Darlene?" I said I thought that was a wonderful idea, as long as we didn't stay too long. Just then Maureen stopped in to say hello, and someone poured her a glass of wine and invited her to join us. Eight women, fortified with chardonnay and merlot, marched down the hall behind me. I opened the door, and warned Daddy, "Prepare for a party, Dad. They came just to see you." Each one gathered around the sides and foot of his bed. He grinned up at them, and I said, "You always did have a way with women, Dad. I bet no other man in the history of Grace Lodge has been in bed with eight gorgeous babes at once!" He nodded and grinned some more.

"Don't give him the wrong idea," Julie admonished. "We're not here to sleep with you, LaVerne. We're here to toast you!"

All eight of us raised our glasses, and Julie said, "To LaVerne, the best father Darlene could have ever had!"

"Cheers, LaVerne!" they chorused while glasses clinked. Daddy's grin expanded to a full-blown smile.

"Oh, take a picture, Maureen, please?" I asked. Phones appeared out of nowhere, and the toast was captured for posterity.

"You need to sing!!" Linda said. "Sing him that lullaby—what's it called? Dunderbeck? The horrible one about the butcher your mom sang to all of you! Sing it!"

All of the W(h)iners knew about this very dark German novelty song which my mother sang to us five children, warping our psyches one by one. Daddy had listened to her sing it many times, and he found it just as amusing as she did. The tale of an unscrupulous butcher whose wife accidentally turns him into sausage while walking in her sleep should have given everyone who ever heard it nightmares, but it was more soothing and familiar to the Machtan kids than "Rockabye, Baby." I wasn't sure how Daddy would feel about hearing a song that ends when Dunderbeck's wife "gave the crank a helluva yank, and Dunderbeck was meat," but I thought I'd give it a go. I started singing softly at first, and as soon as Dad recognized the melody, his eyes opened, his fingers kept time on the blankets, and he began to grin. I pulled out all the stops then, and by the time I finished, we were all laughing. I said, "There you go, Dad. That one was for you." One by one the W(h)iners said their goodbyes and headed back down the hall. When Daddy closed his eyes again, I joined them.

We all passed around the phones so we could see the pictures. "Just look at him," Nan said. "He's so pleased, and so proud of you. And now he knows just how much he and you are loved. I'm so glad we did this." We finished our drinks while they cleaned up and put away the remains of our celebration, handing the unfinished wine to me. Then they left as they had arrived, with long hugs and kisses sealing their love and solidarity. I was sure that no one had ever had better friends than I, and no one had ever had a better sendoff than my father.

Just Like That

Dad's card-playing buddy Jenny stopped in before supper to check on him and me. She had been in and out several times the past few days, and I enjoyed the diversion of her company. She asked me if I had eaten and invited me to join her at dinner, but I assured her I wasn't hungry. After supper, she returned, thrusting her snack stash at me, insisting that I eat something. I told her I would share some of her peanuts and chips, but only if she joined me in a glass of my leftover wine. She settled in, and we chatted quietly, swapping stories of family history throughout the evening and refilling our glasses. I think she would have been there until morning if I hadn't eventually told her I was tired. She gave me a long, warm hug, said good night and that she'd be back in the morning, then toddled off to her room just down the hall. The aides that had come and gone found her nosy and intrusive, but I didn't feel that way at all. It was comforting to have a motherly presence in the room to share my sorrow.

Again, I struggled to find the oblivion of sleep, but it took a long time and was fitful when it came. I kept reliving the events of the past days, weeks, months, years, wondering how I could have done better. I felt lonely and little. I had been reporting Dad's status to Homer via phone calls, but he would still be in Indiana for a few days.

I was looking forward to Ken's arrival in the morning and the emotional support he would bring with him. In the meantime, I strained to hear Dad's breathing and waited once again for morning. I was looking forward to the return of Dad's favorite aide, "Shitbird Jane." She had been off for the last two days. I wondered if he would still recognize her.

Grace Lodge came to life again around 6 a.m. The day shift replaced the night, residents began to stir and head to breakfast, while Daddy slept on. One of the aides urged me to go have breakfast, and when I declined, she said she would have something sent up. Jenny came in again to check on us, and while we were sitting quietly talking, and I picked at a muffin that I didn't want, we heard Jane whistling her way down the hall. She swept in the room, so much more at ease with this situation than I was. She leaned over my Dad, squeezed his hands, and gave him a gentle hug. "Hey, LaVerne," she said. "I'm back. Did ya miss me?" Dad opened his eyes for the first time since the W(h)iners' farewell the evening before. "It's my birthday, LaVerne!! What do you think of that?! I'm so glad I get to spend it with you!" she exclaimed. He said nothing but slowly his characteristic grin moved across his face. "Oh my gosh, LaVerne," she said. "Look at that! There's a shitbird at your feeder!" Jenny and I followed her pointing finger to the red-winged blackbird perched outside, peering in. April sunshine glinted off the spread of glowing scarlet and ebony feathers, and he stared solemnly back at us for a fleeting moment of silence. Then he opened his wings and disappeared into the blue sky of early spring.

"He's gone," Jane said quietly.

"Yes, he is," I agreed.

"No, not the bird," she said. "Your father. I think he just took his last breath." I returned my gaze to her checking for a pulse first in his wrist, then his throat. She felt no heartbeat, and she said again, "He's gone."

"Just like that?" I whispered. "Just like that?"

"He waited until he was ready," Jane said. "He knew you were ready too."

She enfolded me in her arms, and then left to notify Maureen and hospice. Jenny hugged me as well, and then excused herself to give me some time alone with Daddy. I held his still warm hand, kissed his forehead, and whispered, "And flights of angels sing thee to thy rest."

I sat weeping softly beside him, grateful that I had been there when it happened, already missing his quiet, steadfast presence in my life. My eyes kept returning to the feeder, but no winged-creature perched there again that morning.

I don't know how long I sat there beside his bed trying to process the reality of his passing. It probably wasn't long until Maureen came in. She had vacation that day, but she immediately came in to offer her condolences when she got the call. She assured me that the hospice nurse was on her way and would be attending to Dad. The nurse arrived soon after that, extended her sympathies, and said that I was welcome to stay or go as she prepared him for the funeral home's arrival. I was quick to excuse myself, not wanting to witness the indignity of the routines that went with death. I went down the hall and started making phone calls, sharing the news with family and friends. After the first few calls, the nurse came to get me, and we walked back into what had been Daddy's apartment. Now it was just another room, just a place that he had occupied for six months, a place that would soon be filled by someone else. In the meantime, there was much that I needed to do. I was wondering how to begin when Bruce, the owner of the local funeral home handling Daddy's transport to Marshfield, gently knocked at the door. I had known Bruce in a professional capacity for a long time, but this was personal. He enveloped me in his arms and said quietly as he had told countless other bereaved daughters, "I am so sorry for your loss. We will take very good care of your father. Do you want to stay while we move him?"

"No, I can't watch that," I admitted. "I just can't. I loved him so. Please be gentle."

"Of course," Bruce said.

I gave my father a final kiss and turned away so I wouldn't have to witness his last exit from Grace Lodge. I knew that the next time we were together, he would be laid out in the coffin of his choosing in Marshfield, but I simply couldn't watch them zip him into a body bag and carry him away.

When I heard the elevator doors open and close, I returned to his room and sank down into his recliner, alone, waiting for Ken. Shortly after, he walked in the door, a bouquet of roses in his hands. "You just missed him," I said. "He died this morning." Ken looked at the empty bed, handed me the flowers, and said, "I'm so sorry." I am not exactly sure what those words meant. Was he sorry that he had missed Daddy's dying, just like we missed Mom's? Was he sorry that he and Dad had never understood each other or been close? Was he sorry for his loss, or mine, or everyone's? Was he sorry for what lay behind or what lay ahead? I was sorry for all those things, and so many more that remained unidentified, unnamed.

"Let's go home," I told him. "I haven't been there in days, and there are a million things we have to do. I could use some help." I grabbed my coat and purse, turned away from Dad's empty hospital bed, hearing an announcer's voice inside my head echoing, "LaVerne has left the building."

The Devil Is in the Details

There was a flurry of funeral preparations after that. Too many phone calls to count. "I didn't think he was that close to dying," Homer said when I reached him. "I really didn't."

"I really did," I said.

"When's the funeral?" he asked.

"Don't know yet," I said.

"Well, I'll be there," he assured me. "I'm heading home tomorrow."

I hoped by the time he got back, I'd be ready for him. For now, I needed the space of his absence to sort through my feelings and do what needed to be done.

Ken and I met Dale at the funeral home in Marshfield the next day to make arrangements. Most of them were already in place. Mom and Dad had made life easy for us by planning and paying for their funerals, burial plots, and headstones years earlier. Dad had chosen his pallbearers and hymns at my insistence shortly after he moved in with us, and then we never spoke of it again. He wanted his funeral conducted at Immanuel in Marshfield, where he and all his children had been baptized and confirmed. Cliff and Mom's funerals had also been held at Immanuel, much to my chagrin. The services had been cold, impassionate, and mechanical. I was still bitter about both and determined that Dad's would be done right.

I oversaw every detail, even the ones Dale and Ken thought wrong or unimportant. It fell to me to write the obituary, and I was fine with that. Dale and Ken approved of the draft I ran past them. When I asked who would like to do the eulogy, "not-its" were loudly spoken by brothers, in-laws, nephews, and nieces. "You were closest to him; you should be the one to do it," they all kept saying. Although I wasn't sure that I should or could, I knew that no one else was going to step up, so I agreed. But I also said that I was going to invite Dad's son-in-law Richard, an ordained Lutheran minister who Dad thought very highly of, to either co-officiate at the funeral or speak. An "outsider" conducting Dad's funeral at Immanuel was out of the question, the Immanuel minister said, but he and Dale reluctantly agreed to allow Richard time to share memories of the thirteen years Dad had been part of the Noeldner family. Dale would have preferred the Noeldners not be included at all. "This isn't all about you, or us," I argued. "They loved him, and he loved them. They have every right to be there. Dad expected that when he listed them as half of his pallbearers. They are entitled to grieve too." And so, they came, from a few blocks to a thousand miles away, to honor Dad.

I was well satisfied with the funeral home visitation and church service. The flowers were plentiful and beautiful, and the photo collages artfully arranged. I was especially proud of the video of Dad's life that I created. It had been easy to do, since all I simply had to add to the one I had carefully put together for his ninetieth birthday party. It ended with him waving while standing in his glorious gardens of glads. That same photo graces the cover and inspired the title of this memoir. The outpouring of friends and family was gratifying, and my eyes filled with tears when the Grace Lodge activity director Brenda walked in with Jenny. They had come a long way to pay their respects, but they weren't the only ones. The W(h)iners were all there, Nancy, Gordie, Robin, friends and relatives from near and far. It was so supportive and affirming. The Bible readings were appropriate, and the minister's message acceptable. Richard's remembrance of Dad was accurate, amusing, and touching. When it was my turn, I took a deep breath, moved to the pulpit, and tried to convey the essence of my father's lifetime in five hundred words or less. People nodded in the right places, chuckled in the right places, and wiped away tears along with me when I finished.

Sue sang Dad's favorite hymns, "The Old Rugged Cross," "What a Friend We Have in Jesus," and "On Eagle's Wings," as he had requested. The music was beautiful, but by far my favorite was the last song, one which I had also used to end the video. Daddy had never heard it, and I doubted that anyone else had either. It is a gentle ballad that I asked Sue to learn and sing as the sending song. Tears rolled down my face as Sue strummed her guitar and sang, "Way out on the water, a ship is under sail, leaving wavy starlight, and a dreamer in her trail. I wave bye bye. I pray God speed. I wish you lovely weather, more luck than you need. You'll only sail in circles, so there's no need to cry. No, I'll see you again one day, and then I waved bye bye." The Jesse Winchester lyrics said everything I couldn't.

Dad's military honors took place in front of the church rather than at the cemetery, because the burial would be family-only in a few weeks when the ground finally thawed. The uniformed honor guard fired the traditional three rifle volleys, and when the lonely sound of Taps subsided, they ceremoniously folded the casket flag and handed it to Dale. We filed back into the church for the obligatory luncheon, distributed flowers, thanked everyone, and said our goodbyes. Leftover food and thank you note duties were divided among the three of us, awkward hugs exchanged, and then we went our separate ways. I don't know how the others felt, but I was and still am well-satisfied with my father's funeral. That's the one thing for Daddy that I think I did exactly right.

Moving Out

There was little time to rest after returning home. Dad's empty Grace Lodge apartment was costing over $100 a day, and that was a ridiculous waste of money. It needed to be emptied as soon as possible, especially since Maureen had someone else ready to move in. The next day, I gathered boxes, totes, and laundry baskets and headed to Grace Lodge, bracing myself for the task of packing away what was left of Dad.

Since we had already moved Dad's bed and desk out when the hospital equipment was moved in, there wasn't a lot of furniture left to deal with. I had no idea what to do with Dad's lift chair. It was in excellent condition, but we had no place or need for it at our house. The same was true of the lamp next to it. As I was cleaning out his dresser and closets, Maureen stopped in. "How's it going?" she asked.

"It's tough," I said. "I don't know what to do with a lot of this stuff, especially his chair. Is there a resident who might be able to use it?"

"I'll check and get back to you," she said. "For the time being, just leave it where it is."

I appreciated that. It gave me a place to sit when I needed a break from folding and boxing shirts, sweaters, vests, pants, underwear, socks, pajamas…plus the suits, the ties, the jackets, and of course, the coats. Who knew Dad had so many clothes??? My father's scent filled the room, but I knew that it would soon be gone, and I would miss it. Almost everything went to Goodwill, except a worn shirt my cousin Nancy had lovingly patched with an embroidered butterfly, his Honor Flight polo and jacket, and of course, his trademark Columbia parkas. I simply couldn't part with them, and so they went home with me.

Hiding at the bottom of one dresser drawer were Daddy's bingo quarters stashed in a neat little covered glass jar. Nestled next to that was his worn black leather wallet. Inside I found his many insurance cards, his hunting and fishing license, and a copy of his honorable discharge from the Army. In the bill compartment nestled $41 that he would never get another chance to spend. Carefully folded next to the money was a slip of paper on which he had painstakingly written his name and my address and phone number as neatly as his gnarled old arthritic hands would allow. I wondered when he had done that, and exactly why, but it was comforting to know that he had carried me with him. In the picture section was a small version of the last formal family photo we had had taken years before when Mom was still alive. The large rendition was still hanging on his wall. Inside the coin purse nestled a small simple unadorned metal cross that I had never seen, and Dad had never mentioned. In the final slot, I found a copy of a well-worn poem. It read in part, "I carry this cross...a reminder to me...that I am a Christian...wherever I be."

I carefully put everything away as I had found it and tucked Dad's wallet in my purse. I wiped away the tears and blew my nose, then moved on to the bathroom. While I was emptying the medicine chest and linen closet, two men from hospice came in and carted away the hospital bed, wheelchair, commode and other miscellaneous medical supplies that would be delivered to another dying man or woman. It made me sad. But then, almost everything did.

I piled my SUV with box after box of Dad's possessions, made two runs to Goodwill, and then loaded it again with the stuff I would be taking home. I had filled Dad's World War Two Army trunk with keepsakes and photos and bedding that I would return to the room he had occupied at our house. In my mind it would remain "his" room for a long time.

The next day while I was packing the kitchen dishes that Dad had never used, Maureen stopped again. "Wow," she said. "You've made a lot of progress. You're almost finished. I wanted to tell you the tenant who is moving in said that he would appreciate having the chair and lamp if you don't need them. He wants to know how much you're asking."

"That's great," I said. "Tell him he doesn't owe me a thing. That chair is really heavy and a bear to move. I'm just glad I won't have to, and that someone here can use it."

"That's very generous and thoughtful," Maureen said. She paused. "I hate to bring this next thing up after everything else you've been through, but it's kind of important. Some of the residents are asking about your dad, and I'd like to have a brief service here in his memory. It helps both the residents and the staff get some sort of closure. Is that possible? If so, the sooner we can do that, the better. Some are already forgetting who he was, and others are confused about what happened to him."

I thought it was a good idea. I met with Pastor Devon, and he offered to conduct the service. We held it a few days later in the dining room after lunch. Pastor Devon did the readings and sermon, and once more we joined in Daddy's favorite hymns. On behalf of Dad, I thanked the room full of familiar faces for their friendship and care, then sang an acapella song of gratitude. As everyone made their way back to their rooms, the staff lined up for hugs, and then I headed out the door, glad for this second goodbye but relieved that it was over. Despite the urging to come back and visit, I doubted that I would return any time soon. My business here was done, I thought, and I would finally put Grace Lodge behind me. As it turns out, that wasn't meant to happen just yet.

THE RETURN OF SPRING

Letting Go

Spring finally overtook winter, and the snow and ice gradually disappeared in the warming sun. Days and weeks passed, and my life fell into my old routine. I was traveling frequently, again visiting the schools that had waited patiently for my return while I was caring for Dad. When I was home, Homer fell into his pre-Dad patterns as I grieved. I am sure he was grateful to be free of Dad's omnipresence dividing us, but I still felt plenty of resentment about what I regarded as my husband's callousness. I wondered if I would ever be able to let it go.

One windy, sunny day in mid-May, the family gathered again in Marshfield, this time for Dad's interment. As we stood beside the open grave next to Mom's, I thought that this would be the first time they would be together in sixteen years. It was comforting thinking of them sharing the same space for eternity. The funeral director handed each of us bundles of shiny red, white, and blue balloons which bumped in the breeze as the minister presided over a brief graveside service and the lowering of the casket. When it was over, we released the balloons. As I watched them soar up, up, up against the blue sky to the west, I imagined them and Daddy flying over the family farm that had been home. I sang in my head the words of his sending song: "I wave bye bye. I pray God speed. I wish you lovely weather, more luck than you need. You'll only sail in circles, so there's no need to cry. No, I'll see you again one day, and then I waved bye bye."

I'll Fly Away

Time continued to pass, as of course it does. My grief diminished somewhat, but I found Sunday church services to be especially difficult. I sat in the same pew Daddy and I had shared, clutching a Kleenex and fighting tears as I remembered. People were supportive and understanding, but the hole in my heart was huge. Perhaps our lay minister recognized that, and she asked if I would be willing to fill in as a Eucharistic volunteer, visiting older shut-ins and providing them with Communion. I was surprised to be asked and could not come up with a good reason to say no, so I agreed. I would be trained and assigned to two or three congregants in the next month or so, she said.

I had nearly forgotten about it when one day she called me in, presented me with my kit and a crash liturgical Communion course. She also gave me the names and addresses of the people I would be visiting, wished me well, and sent me on my way.

I was nervous about this responsibility, so when I saw that one of my assignments lived in Grace Lodge, I thought I would start there. I at least knew where I was going and would see some familiar faces. I thought I would also make a point of visiting Jenny while there. I was apprehensive about returning to this place of so much emotion, but I was determined to get through it.

I parked in my old familiar space, walked through the doors as I always had, and headed to Maureen's office. It was good to see her. I explained what brought me there and the name of the man I was visiting. "What room is Gene in?" I asked.

She hesitated a minute, then smiled. "I'll walk you there and introduce you," she said. "He's on the second floor."

We walked up the steps, past the elevator and down the hall. We stopped outside Dad's room. She smiled again. "You're kidding," I said.

"Nope," she replied. "Gene moved in right after your dad died." She knocked, introduced us, turned, and left.

Gene was sitting in Dad's recliner, exactly where it had always been. He was a tall, lanky, good looking old man, with glasses and gray hair reminiscent of my father. He had moved into Grace Lodge because his family didn't think he could take care of himself and live alone anymore, he said. He wasn't happy about that, but he was resigned to his situation. At least he had a good view of the river, he added. Déjà vu only begins to describe how weird and wonderful this all felt.

He had been a member of Immanuel since he was a child, but he couldn't manage to attend church anymore, so he was grateful that I had come. We talked for a long time. I learned that Gene was a widower who still missed his wife. He told me about the rest of his family, the house he had lived in and still owned, the work he had done, his retirement, his present interests, and people we had in common. I told him a little about me and a lot about Dad's stay in this same room and how I missed him. Eventually we shared the wafers and wine of Communion, ending as always with the blessing. He thanked me for coming, and as I hugged him goodbye, I told him I would be back soon.

That was the beginning of the story of Gene and

Darlene, a postscript to my life with Dad. I looked forward to my regular visits with Gene, and so did he. As the months passed, Gene's health began to fail, and I watched helplessly and sadly as he traveled the same journey as my father. He lost his mobility, and spent more and more time in the recliner, and then his bed. My pastor knew that I was struggling with this, and she asked if I would like to be reassigned to another parishioner. "No," I said, "it's good for both of us, even if it's hard."

The last time I visited Gene, I could hear people singing downstairs. I asked if he would like me to wheel him to the performance, but he said he wasn't up to it, and he could listen from his room. We chatted, prayed, shared Communion, hugged and said our goodbyes. As I headed out the door, I slowed to listen to the song. Then I stopped dead in my tracks. This is what I heard: "Some glad mornin' when this life's over, I'll fly away." Alfred E. Brumley wrote his hymn "I'll Fly Away" in 1929, but I had never heard it before. As I listened, I remembered Daddy's final morning, and the red-winged blackbird on whose wings he had departed.

There are those who believe in coincidence, happenstance, and randomness. I am not one of them. I believe my father sent this message of love and comfort to me. It brought the peace and healing I had been seeking, and it is the final chapter in this story, although I miss him still. I miss his voice, his grin. I miss him spring, summer, fall, and winter. I see him everywhere I look. Every single day. Our journey together was fraught with joy and sorrow, and there was nothing easy about it. But I wouldn't have missed it. I was, and am, so blessed to have been part of Daddy's long goodbye.

(In)Visibility

They warned that you were leaving
but the six months they gave you
Turned to nine, to twelve, to twenty
and I thought perhaps you—
a man of few words
whose crooked smile and gnarled hands
did all the talking for him—
were here to stay.
When you finally slipped away
that April morning,
I felt nothing
because you were suddenly nothing.
But not for long.
There you are again
in the form of red-winged blackbirds,
warm fires, gladiola, waving American flags.
Not a day passes without you.
In my sleeping and in my waking
in my yesterdays and tomorrows
everywhere I look—there you are.
I am so very grateful for
the presence
of your absence.

About the Author

Darlene Machtan is a daughter, a wife, a sister, a teacher, and a writer. Her experience coping with the care giving of her father is one many others have had or will have. She has published a companion memoir, *Conversations With My Mother*, as well as three poetry chapbooks. She lives in Northern Wisconsin with her husband, three dogs, and countless memories of her father.

Acknowledgements

The danger of thanking others for their help in a project of this scope is leaving someone out. Still, I would be remiss if I didn't express gratitude to the following for their contributions in the creation of this book. In alphabetical order, thank you to:
- Nan Andrews, for using her magic to transform a manuscript into the final product which you are reading;
- Beta readers Nan, Terri Angell, Pastor Tammy Barthels, Beth Bloom, Julie Bronson, Renea Dettman, Wayne Gagnon, Linda Goldsworthy, Trisha Hansen, Karen Kitze, Ken Machtan, Martin Machtan, Garyn Roberts, Jane Roe, Mark Spatafore, and Lisa Young for feedback from organization to photos to comma placement and everything in between;
- Maureen O'Melia and the entire Grace Lodge assisted living staff for the wonderful care they provided my father in the final months of his life;
- Homer Van Meter, who sacrificed much on Daddy's and my behalf;
- The W(h)iners, my steadfast supporters before, during, and after Daddy's Long Goodbye

And finally, to Daddy, without whom there would have been no story, and no me.

Christmas card, 2012